The
PEACE of the PRESENT

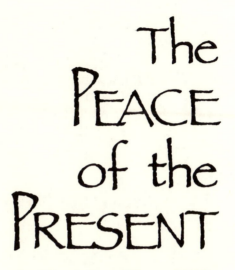

The PEACE of the PRESENT

An Unviolent Way of Life

John S. Dunne

UNIVERSITY OF NOTRE DAME PRESS
NOTRE DAME   LONDON

Library of Congress Cataloging-in-Publication Data

Dunne, John S., 1929–
    The peace of the present: an unviolent way of life /
John S. Dunne.
       p.   cm.
    Includes bibliographical references and index.
    ISBN 0-268-01586-4
    1. Nonviolence — Religious aspects — Christianity.
I. Title.
BT736.6.D86   1990
241'.697 — dc20   90-70853
                                           CIP

Contents

Preface   ix

1. The Ways of Desire   1
   The End of Desire
   The Beginning of Desire

2. Violent and Unviolent Ways   22
   Violent Origins
   Purpose and Cross-Purpose
   Peaceful Ends

3. Waiting on Love   51
   "If there is no love, what then?"
   "Love is a direction"

4. The Peaceable Kingdom   71
   "The heart desires too much"
   "The hidden harmony is better . . ."

5. The Sense of "I" in Christianity   92
   "I am": A Conversation with David Daube
   "I will die": A Conversation with René Girard
   The Sense of "I": A Conversation with Erik Erikson
   "Christ dwells in you as you"

6. The Peace of the Present   102

Notes   115

Index   133

You are a councillor: if you can command these elements to silence and work the peace of the present, we will not hand a rope more; use your authority. If you cannot, give thanks you have lived so long, and make yourself ready in your cabin for the mischance of the hour, if it so hap.—Cheerly, good hearts!—Out of our way, I say.

—Boatswain to Gonzalo in Shakespeare's *Tempest* (act 1, scene 1, lines 19–25)

Preface

We may think we are in one story when all along we are in another. I may think, for instance, I am in a story that is already over, and there is nothing more to hope of life, when in reality the story is going on, and some important thing is still to come. What I think I want of life and what I truly want may not be the same. It is the difference between mimetic desire, wanting what I see others want, and heart's desire, living clear down in my heart, even between violence, hardening my heart, and nonviolence, living heart to heart.

Living clear down in my heart, as I conceive it, living heart to heart, means living in "the peace of the present," an expression I have taken from the first scene of Shakespeare's *Tempest*, "the peace of the presence"[1] according to another reading, the royal presence, for me the presence of God. It means living in the presence in the present. I imagine it as living in the peaceful eye of the storm. It means living really in two worlds, in the adventurous world of time and in the serene world of eternity. ". . . and a great stillness came upon him," Tolkien tells of an adventurer who lived in two worlds, "and he seemed to be both in the World and in Faery, and also outside them and surveying them, so that he was at once in bereavement, and in ownership, and in peace."[2] In life it is similar, I think, a great peace comes upon us when we realize we are not only in a story of separation from one another and from God but in a story of union too and reunion, and we are also outside and telling the story. It comes when we are at the still point where two worlds meet and there is one story.

It was the story of war that originally led me to embrace nonviolence. I was working on my first book, *The City of the Gods*, and was following the story of war from *The Iliad* to *War and Peace*. What struck me was the seeming absurdity of war, the violent clash of purpose and cross-purpose leading not to the realization of a higher purpose but simply to mutual destruction. I had thought earlier that by making a distinction between limited and total war I could discern between rational and irrational forms of warfare, as Augustine did between just and unjust war.[3] The absurdity I found, though, seemed to undermine any conception of a rational war. I read the *Bhagavad-Gita* too and found there, as in the title scene of *War and Peace* where Prince Andre lay looking up into the infinite peaceful sky in the midst of battle, the thought of living in peace in the midst of war.

I embraced nonviolence as a way of life, of living in peace in the midst of conflict, more than as a technique of resolving conflict. I was invited three times to Chile over the years to speak about all this. I say "all this," though it was only the last time I went, a year ago, that I actually called my talks a seminar "on the spirituality of nonviolence." It is one thing to do something, another to know what you are doing, and still another to name it. The first time I came to Santiago was in 1968 during the presidency of Frei and the democracy, a time of hope. I spoke of a way of living your life in your times, balancing an awareness of your life with an awareness of your times. The second time was in 1978, ten years later, during the dictatorship of Pinochet, a time of despair and desperation. I spoke of a way of following the heart, living in uncertainty without despairing. The third time was again after an interval of ten years, in 1988 at the year's end, after the plebiscite in which the people voted "No" to the dictatorship, a time of renewed hope. I spoke of the spirituality of nonviolence while my friend Diego Irarrázaval spoke of the situation in Latin America. Although we spoke of nonviolence as a way of life, it was the successful use of nonviolence in the plebiscite, I think, that gave force to what we were saying.

Here in this book, started before and finished after those

last talks in Chile, I write of "an unviolent way of life." I start with "the ways of desire." René Girard has it that desire is mimetic, we desire what we see others desire, and violence too is mimetic, we do unto others as has been done unto us. A person who has been abused in growing up, for instance, is likely to become an abuser, unless the cycle of violence is somehow broken. I want to say there is a heart's desire, nevertheless, a desire to know and be known, to love and be loved, and I want to link nonviolence with heart's desire as Girard links violence with mimetic desire. Instead of simply renouncing desire along with violence, as he does, I propose to follow the heart's desire. When I write of "violent and unviolent ways" then, I speak of the numbing of the heart that takes place on the violent way, "psychic numbing" as Robert Jay Lifton calls it, and the kindling of the heart and the illumining of the mind that takes place on the unviolent way. I speak of "waiting on love," how the heart's longing becomes love, and of "the peaceable kingdom," of union and reunion in a kingdom of hearts.

A further insight came to me when I returned from Chile and was preparing an inaugural lecture I was to give at Notre Dame. It was that the sense of "I" is the locus of peace. I had intended to speak of "an endless conversation" of faith and faith, of faith and reason, and of faith and conscience. My sister said "Why not use actual conversations?" So I wrote down three conversations, one I had with David Daube, one with René Girard, and one with Erik Erikson. After writing them out, I realized all three had to do with the sense of "I" in Christianity. So that became the theme of the lecture. Then in writing the book I realized the true saying of "I" goes with the kindling of the heart and the false with the numbing of the heart. The true saying of "I" is the password into the kingdom of hearts.

My thanks go to my sister, Carrin Dunne, to Bill Lewers and Tim Scully and the Holy Cross Fathers in Chile, to Diego Irarrázaval, to Helen Luke, to Robert Jay Lifton, to David Daube, René Girard, and Erik Erikson. I wish also to remember here Father John A. O'Brien, a friend of many years ago, in whose name I received a chair of theology at Notre Dame and gave my inaugural lecture on the sense of "I" in Christianity on April 18, 1989. Also I am grateful to friends, not named here, whose words I have quoted from conversation and from letters. Each time I have been to Chile I have traveled also to Peru and to the heights of Macchu Picchu,[4] and that is where this book begins, in peace among the ruins.

1

The Ways of Desire

— Nicanor Parra

On my way north, twenty years ago, I stopped at the ruins of Macchu Picchu, Inca city of refuge in the Andes, and I stood alone there, high up in the sunset, watching the llamas come down into the plaza below me and settle in a circle for the night. As the sun set and the twilight changed, I almost expected the people too of the Incas to return. I left finally in the dark to find my own bed around the other side of the mountain. Then early in the morning I came out again to see the sunrise, though the high horizons of the Andes were clouded. I felt disappointed, but I waited, hoping the clouds would break. I waited on for an hour, and then the clouds did part and I could see the sun had not yet risen over the mountains tops, that it was just about to appear. Then its bright edge did show, and the first ray, as it seemed to me, struck the strangely shaped stone at my feet that was, I learned afterwards, a sundial, and then the sunlight spread through the ruins of the city. As the sun rose, the llamas rose too, and my heart rose within me. I knew there was life here and hope, there was resurrection from the dead.

Our heart's desire is for life and light and love. I could feel it at that sunrise that was also heartrise. We desire to know and be known, to love and be loved. Yet there is a flaw, I could see it in the ruins that were revealed in the sunlight, for "The lonely of heart is withered away."[1] The fairy child sings this in Yeats's play, *The Land of Heart's Desire.* In fact, in the original version of the play the child also sings "The lonely of heart must wither away."[2] That is how we experience the heart's desire, it seems, as a loneliness of heart, a loneliness that is at once an aloneness

1

and a longing for union and reunion, a loneliness that withers the heart if it remains unrequited. There is something of that withering away to be seen at Macchu Picchu, I thought, in the ruins, in the sense of a grandeur that once was and is no longer, in the feeling for the presence of the dead.

Is this withering away something the heart itself seeks, desiring a "maddening freedom," as Yeats says, a "bewildering light"?[3] There is adventure in "maddening freedom" and "bewildering light," but there is no serenity, no peace. There is a serenity in the sunrise, on the other hand, a peace in the heartrise, as if some great fear were overcome. What do we fear? The very same things we desire, it seems, to know and be known, to love and be loved. The sunrise is an illumining, not a bewilderment of light; the heartrise is a kindling, not a madness of freedom, just because of the serenity, just because of the peace, just because the fear is overcome. "Desire is always reflection on desire,"[4] René Girard says, meaning that we see what others desire and we desire to have it too, that we are always miming the desires of others. Yet there is a still more inward interplay in desire, I think, between desire and fear: we fear what we desire and we desire what we fear; we see dread in the shadow of fascination and fascination in the shadow of dread, but the spell is broken in the sunrise that is heartrise when we awaken to the heart's desire.

There is the one heart's desire, I want to say, and there are the many ways of desire, the many paths of the labyrinth where the heart can be lost. Finding the true way is a matter of discerning between heart's desire and mimetic or competitive desire, between what we truly want and what we think we want, seeing what others want. The many passageways of the labyrinth, the blind alleys, the dead ends, make it difficult to find the way from the interior to the entrance and from the entrance to the center. The center I will call "the end of desire" and the entrance I will call "the beginning of desire." If all desire is mimetic, as Girard says, then the center has to be a peace that comes of renunciation. If there is heart's desire, as I am saying, then it is a peace that comes of fulfillment.

The End of Desire

I stopped at Macchu Picchu again, ten years later, this time during the day, at high noon in fact, and just sat in a quiet spot I found, looking out over the valley and the river below, contemplating the mountains, the setting where the Incas had fled from the conquering Spaniards, the secluded world with its high mountain walls, narrow in its compass, great in its height and depth. Most of the adventure this time was simply in coming and going on the little train that runs through the river valley between Cuzco and Macchu Picchu. The time here in the ruins was uneventful but filled with peace. That is what I found this second time, I think, an eternal peace, indeed a sense of time filled with eternity, as if the ruins spoke of time and passing while the mountains and the valley, the river and the sunshine spoke of eternity and enduring.

Is contemplation the end of desire? I find nothing in my diary about this second visit to Macchu Picchu except this, "Contemplation: I spent a long time yesterday sitting in the ruins of Macchu Picchu, looking at the mountains, and asking the Lord for comfort and counsel." I wrote this to contrast with the events I was witnessing on the following day, "Action: we saw the teachers on strike marching down a street in Lima, and we saw the police cordoning off the main square in Lima." It is usual for philosophers right now to consider desire as an element of action along with belief: if you did not take a certain course of action it was because you did not really want to, on balance, or did not believe you would, did not see yourself doing it. When it comes to the goal of desire a paradox arises in this kind of thinking, "the end of desire should be the end of desire,"[5] that is, in desiring we desire the elimination of our desire. The paradox vanishes, however, if we consider contemplation as something distinct from action. Then the end of desire is not just no desire, no action. It is contemplation. We end not simply in desirelessness but in knowing and being known, in loving and being loved.

Still, it may be that we come to fulfillment only through

the renunciation. Charles Williams tells a story about a stone called "The End of Desire." The stone is like the fabulous philosopher's stone of alchemy, able to turn base metals into gold, and to cure all diseases, and to prolong life indefinitely, but it destroys anyone who comes to it without a pure heart. In the end only a man who is transformed by the courage of selfless action, a woman who is transformed by willing endurance of suffering, and a simple man whose only desire is to "fulfil good as he knew it" become "capable of receiving under those conditions the End of Desire."[6] So in the story the paradox is upheld, the end of desire is the end of desire, but in a profound sense, not just that desire seeks its own elimination but that the renunciation of desire means the fulfillment of desire. It is like the insight that Dietrich Bonhoeffer came to when he was in prison and deprived of all the things he would normally desire, "We can have abundant life, even though many wishes remain unfulfilled."[7]

It is abundant life, I want to say too, rather than the fulfillment of wishes that is the heart's desire. "There are two tragedies in life," George Bernard Shaw says. "One is to lose your heart's desire. The other is to gain it."[8] He is speaking of our wishes, our frustration when they are unfulfilled, our disappointment when they are fulfilled. But what of abundant life? Again there are two tragedies. One is to have your heart's desire and not realize it. The other is not to have it and think you have. Let us see what it would mean then to discover your heart's desire.

Desire does become reflection on desire when you reflect on your particular way in life, on losing and gaining, on having and not having your heart's desire. Say I feel some misgiving about the road I am taking in life and some regret about a road I am not taking. My misgiving is fear of what I will meet on the road, fear really of death, for death does await me there if I commit my whole life to that way. My regret is a feeling that I am missing out on what I might have had on another way, missing out on what others are enjoying. There is the play of desire with desire, of "a mime called desire,"[9] in my regret, wanting what others want, wanting to have what others have, but there is the more subtle play of desire with fear in my misgiving, as if by taking another way I could somehow evade death. There is an illusion here, an illusion that can be dispelled only by a *memento mori*, a reminder of my mortality, a "remember to die," as if I might forget and go on living forever. When I seriously consider taking another way, then it too opens up before me all the way to death, and I do then remember to die.

As I remember to die, I remember also to live; my life opens up before me and behind me, its meaning begins to emerge, the adventure, the serenity. I remember to love, my deepest feelings come back to me. "Your father loves you," Tolkien has the wise man say to the prince, "and will remember it ere the end."[10] My eyes do become clear when I remember to die, when I remember to live, when I remember to love. I see what matters and what doesn't matter. I am able to discern my heart's desire. It is indeed possible to forget to love, to lose touch with my deepest feelings, when I am caught up in mimetic desire, in competition with others. Then my feelings of what others desire override my own feelings, my love is only rivalry in love, my work only rivalry in work. When I remember, I lose the complexity that comes of competition over someone, over something, and I gain the simplicity, the intensity of willing one thing: not someone or something to *have* so much as someone or something to *be*.

It is true, there is not only memory in this *memento mori* but also understanding and will. Or there is not just a remembering of death but a remembering of life and light and love. Consider last wills and testaments, where people are thinking about these things, about dying and about having and about giving. It is possible, you can see there, to face the prospect of death without letting go of the rivalry in love and in work that may have filled your life, to tighten your grip instead, or to try and extend a hand over the future, if not the *mortmain* of law, still a dead hand. It is possible, on the other hand, even though I am still held by the conviction "I am what I have,"[11] to embrace dying, to let go of having, to give away all that I have. It is possible, beyond that, to differentiate between having and being, to remember the miracle of being, the wonder of my existence, the wonder I felt already as a child before coming to have the many things that are now the main business of my having, and thus to go from the world just as I came into it, naked in my existence.

"Give away all that thou hast," says an old Greek maxim, "then shalt thou receive."[12] When I do let go of everyone and everything, I find I still am, even though I had thought "I am what I have." I learn rather that I am apart from what I have. It is as though my own being is given to me when I give away all I have, and so it is that I receive. I exchange having for being, and when I do I come to understand abundant life. It is not that someone or something was there and now is there no longer. Rather it is my relationship with everyone and everything that has changed, my relationship with the things of my life and above all my relationship with myself. I have gone from "I am what I have" to "I am what I am." That last sentence seems an echo of Exodus 3:14, I AM WHAT I AM, almost as if there were in this a merging with God, a union or reunion with God. Abundant life, if this is so, is a nakedness of being that is infinitely rich.

There is a name for this, "a new name," in the New Testament. Like all the passages of life, my passing from having to being can mean acquiring a name for myself. You can tell the story of your life by naming your names, starting with the nicknames of childhood, going through the use of first name, of middle name, of last name at different times of life, and coming to the titles of age and achievement. The new name in the New Testament, Simon becoming Peter, Saul becoming Paul, is a name of being:

> And for each God has a different response. With every man He has a secret — the secret of a new name. In every man there is a loneliness, an inner chamber of peculiar life into which God only can enter.[13]

These words of George MacDonald seem to say the new name is linked with the deep loneliness we all feel, a loneliness that is not taken away even in the most intimate human relations, and with the longing in that loneliness, the heart's longing. They seem to say the heart's desire cannot be fulfilled except by God, since God alone can enter into that inner chamber of the heart.

God is the end of desire, according to this, and the place in my heart where God only can enter is the mystery of my being. If there were no place like this, if others could enter into any place in my heart, then Jean-Paul Sartre's dictum would hold true, "I am what I have," and there would be nothing I could not give away. I could tell all. My life would be like Sartre's, "the words"[14] I use or have used to communicate what I have to others. If there is a place, on the other hand, where God only can enter, then there is something incommunicable in all my communication, something untold in all my telling. Although I can speak of this place, as MacDonald did, as I am dong now, I cannot make it available to another. Rather I point to a similar place in the other's heart, a place known to the other as mine is to me. It is a place that is known to us when we feel the loneliness of the human condition, when we feel the longing of the heart.

It is at once universal and particular, this place, common and personal. "Everyone has in him something precious that is in no one else," the Baal Shem Tov says, "everyone" and yet "no one else." "But this precious something is revealed to him," Martin Buber adds, "only if he truly perceives his strongest feeling, his central wish, that in him which stirs his inmost being."[15] It is in everyone, for it is the common loneliness of the human condition, but it is loneliness nonetheless, a feeling of being alone and longing to be unalone. It is our strongest, that is, our most fundamental feeling, I think — our central wish, that in us which stirs our inmost being. We can understand one another in our loneliness because we all have it within us, and yet we cannot take it away from one another, cannot make one another unalone, and in that sense cannot enter into that lonely place in one another. God only, according to this, can make us unalone, and that is what it means to say God only can enter into that place in our hearts. In the ending of desire then, God is our strongest feeling, God is our central wish, God is that in us which stirs our inmost being.

All the same, this feeling, this wish, this stirring takes a particular form in each life and leads to the particular way that is truly ours in life. I am not thinking of the many forms of "metaphysical desire," as Girard calls it, "such as the love of risk, thirst for the infinite, stirrings of the poetic soul, *amour fou,* and so on,"[16] so much as the embodiment of desire in the personal relations and the chosen work of a life. If I am heart and soul in the personal relations of my life, if I am heart and soul in my chosen work in life, I come to be heart and soul in a relation with God. It is as if I were spending my life learning to love with all my heart and all my soul. "Unless devotion is given to a thing which must prove false in the end," Charles Williams says, "the thing that is true in the end cannot enter."[17] Unless devotion is given to the finite, to the human, I think he is saying, the infinite, the divine cannot enter.

Must the finite, the human prove false in the end? Only to divine longings, to infinite expectations. It is still the entrance through which "the thing that is true in the end" must enter. It is the finite expression of the infinite, the human revelation of the divine. When MacDonald speaks of the place in us where only God can enter, he goes on to speak of the place in God where only we can enter, a unique place for each person:

> There is a chamber also — (O God, humble and accept my speech) — a chamber in God Himself, into which none can enter but the one, the individual, the peculiar man — out of which chamber that man has to bring revelation and strength for his brethren. This is that for which he was made — to reveal the secret things of the Father.[18]

So the lonely place in us is "not the innermost chamber." There is a further, a deeper chamber, the place in God who is within us, the place where only we can enter, each of us into our own. Yet what we find here can be shared with others. So the finite is the key to the infinite, the human to the divine, each person to something in God that is available to no one else except through that one. Every one of us then, by love and by work, becomes a doorway through which others can come to the end of desire.

"To love and to work," *Lieben und arbeiten,* is Freud's formula, his answer when he was asked "what a normal person should be able to do well."[19] He may have meant love and work are the basic realities of life, are all life has to offer. I want rather to say love and work are the basic symbols of life, the basic expressions of the heart's desire. Love expresses the secret in us, our aloneness and our longing for union and reunion; work expresses the secret in God, the thing in God we have access to, the thing we can bring to bear on the loneliness and the longing. "To love and to work" is a formula of balance, as Freud meant it, guiding us away from a life that is all work without love as well as from a life that is all love and human relations without achievement. The secret in us and the secret in God are linked, I want to say too, for without the loneliness we have no feeling for the thing we discover in God and without the discovery our loneliness goes unrequited.

"One can but have one's heart and hands full, and mine are," Anna Jameson wrote in 1841. "I have love and work enough to last me the rest of my life."[20] Are love and work then enough? Enough to fill a life, I would say, but not enough to fulfill the heart's desire. If the deep loneliness of our heart is not taken away even in the most intimate human relations, then love is not enough, and if the spark of life or light or love we discover and share with others serves only to whet our appetite for life and light and love, then work is not enough. There is need of what Robert Jay Lifton calls "symbolic immortality,"[21] for a fruitfulness of love in sons and daughters who live on after our death, for a fruitfulness of work that outlasts our lifetime in its influence, for a sense of participation in a reality that is greater than ourselves. It is an immortality that is more even than symbolic, I believe, in which we ourselves live on in our children, in our influence, in the reality that is greater than ourselves, not merely as the dead hand of the past but as life and light and love.

Say my heart and my hands are full. Say I do have love and work enough to last me the rest of my life. There is a turn I have to complete, nevertheless, from having to being, an emptying of my heart, an opening of my hands. It is like the letting go of everyone and everything that takes place in dying. If I can do it, I can be life and light and love rather than a dead hand. "Letting be" and "openness to the mystery," Martin Heidegger calls it, where mystery is "that which shows itself and at the same time withdraws."[22] There is a letting be in love that opens me to the mystery of aloneness in me and in the other. There is a letting be in work that opens me to the mystery of the divine spark in me, the heart of my "mystery" in the old sense of a trade and the secrets of a trade. There is a revealing and at the same time a withdrawing. The mystery shows itself and at the same time withdraws and hints of more.

It is the withdrawing that hints of immortality. I come upon something in myself that cannot be exhausted in love and work, something "as inaccessible as God or thou."[23] It is accessible and inaccessible. Letting the mystery be in myself, in God, in the other, I gain access to it after all. Openness to the mystery becomes contemplation, becomes vision. It becomes, like my experience at Macchu Picchu, a vision of eternal peace. It is true, describing the end of desire as mystery, as something accessible and inaccessible, I may seem to be describing only desire itself, how it always goes for the impossible and as soon as someone or something becomes attainable it turns to someone or something else. As long as we think only in terms of likeness it seems so, desire in imitation of desire, love in rivalry with love, work in rivalry with work. As soon as we begin to think in terms of presence, however, it seems otherwise — the presence of God, I mean, the presence of the other, my own presence to myself. It is presence that "shows itself and at the same time withdraws." The mystery is of presence.

Likeness and presence are two ways of thinking about being and knowing as well as desiring. Consider the phrase "alone with the Alone" (*solus cum solo*). There is likeness here and presence. If I am alone with God, I am like God in being alone, and yet being present to God and God to me, being with God, makes me unalone. So too if I know myself as alone, I come to know God as the Alone, and yet being with God, I come to know myself and God as "I and thou." And so too if I desire to be alone, I may be desiring myself, falling in love with my own likeness (Freud's narcissism), or I may be only pretending to desire myself in order to be desirable to others (Girard's coquetry), and yet I may really desire to be alone with God, to be unalone, to be "all one." There is paradox here. Yet likeness, being like, knowing like, desiring like, yields to presence, it seems to me, to being, to knowing, to desiring.

If the end of desire is likeness, we always come in the end to "Like, and yet unlike." One human being is like and yet unlike another. A human being is like and yet unlike God. So if my desire is to be like another person, to be like God, I will end in likeness and unlikeness. If the end of desire is presence, on the other hand, we come in the end to "I and thou," to knowing and being known, to loving and being loved. We are present to one another. We are in the presence of God. Still, the mystery "shows itself and at the same time withdraws," that is to say is "like and yet unlike." So if my desire is for union with another person, if it is for union with God, I can attain my desire only if presence is presence not just in likeness but also in unlikeness. Union with God is presence. Likeness and unlikeness are ways to God, likeness the affirmative way, starting from our likeness to God and ending in what God is like, unlikeness the negative way, starting from our unlikeness to God and ending in our unknowing. The presence of God is there, I want to say, not only in our light but also in our darkness.

What then is the point of likeness and unlikeness? It is the beginning of desire. There was a moment in Thomas Merton's life when he found himself in the position I have been describing, wanting to be alone with God (he had moved from a monastery to a hermitage), and yet wanting to be unalone (he had fallen in love with a young woman who was his nurse when he was in the hospital). Most of his friends were filled with misgivings, but one, the Chilean poet Nicanor Parra, encouraged him, saying one must "follow the ecstasy."[24] The feeling of being accessible and yet inaccessible, of being alone and yet unalone, of being like and yet unlike, brought him not to the end but to the beginning of a road. Although he was near the end of his life, he was not dying but following the ecstasy.

The Beginning of Desire

To follow the ecstasy is to live the paradox of our aloneness and our longing for union and reunion. It is to follow "the road of the union of love with God."[25] It does not mean turning away from death so much as letting go of everyone and everything, instead of everyone and everything being taken away, one by one. Pablo Neruda, another Chilean poet, climbed the heights of Macchu Picchu to escape the one kind of death, where all is taken away, little by little, and to find the other kind, where there is a letting go of all, to go from "dying of my own death,"[26] as he says, to following the ecstasy of life. I had not read Neruda's poem when I was here before, twenty years ago and ten years ago, but only now, on my third visit. This time I have come in the rainy season rather than in the dry, and the scene is a clearing among the clouds at the tops of the mountains. I think of stories where "the meaning of an episode," as Joseph Conrad says, "was not inside like a kernel but outside, enveloping the tale which brought it out only as a glow brings out a haze."[27] The meaning is not in the ruins, in death that is, but in the enveloping sense of mystery.

It is not a matter of the things of life and their passing so much as our relation to the things and our relation to their passing. It is the difference between holding on and letting go, between things being wrested, one by one, from our grasp and things being released. Is desire itself then, grasping desire as in Buddhist doctrine, the cause of wasting death? Desire "invariably goes off in search of a mirage that will increase its lack rather than remedy it," Girard says. "Desire will little by little make any form of satisfaction or even communication with the loved person quite impossible — desire proceeds in the direction of dissociation, decomposition and death."[28] Mimetic desire, that is, not heart's desire, I would say—desire before it knows what it desires, before it turns from the mirage to the mystery.

There is a way, like climbing the heights of Macchu Picchu, that leads from mimetic to heart's desire, from what we think we want to what we truly want. Say I think I want to be in love like others; I want to find, like Merton in love, "the person whose name I would try to use as magic to break the grip of awful loneliness on my heart."[29] There is a way for me, nevertheless, a climb to the heights or a descent to the depths "of awful loneliness" where I find my own true name, a climb or a descent that is essential for me if I am to let the other be other than just an answer to my own loneliness, if I am to live in openness to the mystery of the other. I find "a new name" there or, as Merton came to believe, "I become fully able to realize what I cannot know."[30] Mimetic desire is desiring what I know, what I see everyone else desiring, but not knowing what I desire, what I truly want. Heart's desire, on the other hand, is desiring what I do not know, a life, a light, a love that is greater than myself, and yet knowing what I desire, being in touch with my deepest longings. It is desiring "to realize what I cannot know."

To realize the mystery is to find presence not only in likeness but also in unlikeness, not only in knowing but also in unknowing. What is more, if my heart's desire is to realize, to find presence, the presence of God, of the other, of me to myself, I have to resolve the conflict between like and unlike, between what I *want* to be and what I *have* to be, that is, or rather between what I think I want to be and what I think I have to be. Let us see if on some deep level the person I truly want to be and the person I truly have to be meet in the person I am *meant* to be.

It is by imitation that we learn to act, to speak, to think, it is true, and so also to desire. There is a point, nevertheless, when we pass from doing what others do to doing what we do, from saying what others say to saying what we say, from thinking what others think to thinking what we think, and so also from desiring what others desire to desiring what we desire. Bach is said to have learned musical forms in this way, first doing imitations of the work of others and then composing his own. There is something that can come between imitation and originality, though, and that is failure, the discovery that we are not able to do everything others can do. It can lead us then to find what we can do and others cannot. "Every one of us is something that the other is not," MacDonald says, "and therefore knows some-thing—it may be without knowing that he knows it—which no one else knows."[31] When I come upon the element of depriva-tion in my life, what others can do and I cannot, what others can be and I cannot, I come upon the conflict between what I want to be and what I have to be, but when I come upon what I am and others are not, what I know and others do not, I come upon my personal destiny.

Say I carry imitation to what for me is its highest or deep-est level, the imitation of Christ. Rodin said that if you substi-tute the word "sculpture" for the name "Jesus" wherever it occurs in *The Imitation of Christ* by Thomas à Kempis, it all still holds true.[32] So also, it could be said, if you substitute the word "love." Imitation on this highest or deepest level means being heart and soul in pursuit of the beloved image. It means devotion to Jesus, to work, to love. The imitation is in this, that we become what we know and love. If I devote myself to Christ, then Christ be-comes my life. If I devote myself to sculpture, then sculpture becomes my life. In each instance, "purity of heart is to will one thing."[33] The difference is in the "one thing" that is willed. It is the difference between devoting myself to the wholeness of life, embodied in a whole human being, and devoting myself to a part of life, such as work or love.

If I have devoted myself to one part of life, say my work, it can seem to me all I need for wholeness is to devote myself also to the other part of "love and work," namely love. "When he said love and work," Erik Erikson says of Freud, "he meant a general work productiveness which would not preoccupy the individual to the extent that he might lose his right or capacity to be a sexual and a loving being."[34] As I think of it, that is just what I seem to have lost in devoting myself to my work. Yet when I open myself to love, when I pursue the possibility of love, I seem to come to a divided life, divided between love and work, rather than a wholeness. As I think of "love and work," I think of other formulas such as "prayer and work" and "love and death." There are other elements in life, I can see, not just love to balance off work but also prayer, not just work to balance off love but also death or the capacity for death. The unity of life does not appear in these formulas of balance until I manage to strike the balance. There is a simplicity about wholeness, the quality of a simple life, that I have yet to attain.

Or maybe it is a simplicity that is already there and I have only to embrace it. There is a Vedantic formula for this embracing of your own simplicity, namely, "getting rid of what you haven't got." The complexity of what you haven't got vanishes, according to this, before the simplicity of what you have. If I get rid of the love that I haven't got, I discover the love that I have and I come to realize that my life is not loveless after all. "We get rid of what is not — what we don't have — not what we have," it is said. "In Vedantic philosophy there is nothing to be done; the only important thing is understanding."[35] Thus for me there is nothing to be done about love in my life; the only important thing is to understand the love that is there. Still, it seems to me, there is one thing to be done, and that is to embrace that love. It is not enough to understand it is there unless I am willing, unless I say Yes.

"Through understanding comes liberation,"[36] it is said. And so it does if I make understanding the guide of my life, if understanding leads to will. I am a whole human being, and I am called to wholeness, but I am also a part of a larger reality, and I am called to participation. To realize my wholeness is primarily a matter of understanding; to realize my participation, on the other hand, is primarily a matter of will, of actually participating and not just observing. Love and work are both ways of participating, of being caught up in a larger reality. It is essential for love that I become aware of my own wholeness. Otherwise being caught up in love is going to mean living in dependency on the ones I love. It is essential also for work. Otherwise work is going to mean living in dependency on the things I do. "Whom do you

love?" "What do you do?" These can be questions tantamount
to "Who are you?" "What are you?" if I am unaware of my own
wholeness. Still, I am called to participation, and I can feel the
desire to be caught up in a reality greater than myself. Is wholeness or is participation my heart's desire?

I feel the desire for wholeness as a longing for serenity; I
feel the desire for participation, on the other hand, as a longing
for adventure. "There are two ways of escaping the pain and despair of life, and of the rarest, most subtle dangerous and ensnar-
ing gift that life can bring us, relationship with another person —
love," H.D. says. "One way is to kill that love in one's heart. To
kill love — to kill life. The other is to accept that love, to accept
the snare, to accept the pricks, the thistle."[37] The one way, that
of renunciation, is to try and go directly for wholeness. The other,
that of acceptance of love, of life, is to go to wholeness by way
of participation. I can rest in my own wholeness, but something
in me wants to take part in what is happening in the world, to
come into my wholeness by love, as H.D. says, or better, by love
and by work, by prayer and by work, by love and by death.

I come here to the imitation of Christ, to following his way.
"Was it not necessary that the Christ should suffer these things
and enter into his glory?"[38] Are "these things" not "the pain and
despair of life"? I long for adventure, and yet I long also for serenity. I sit here by myself, let us say, longing for someone to
come into my life and change it and make me a new person,
and yet I long to be free of that longing, to be at peace with myself and with others and with God. Letting be, if I let myself
be lonely as I am, if I let others be for themselves and not just
for me, if I let God be for me as no other can be, leads into a
serenity that does not "kill love," it seems to me, that does not
"kill life." Openness to the mystery, however, if I remain open
to the mystery of my own loneliness, if I remain open to the mystery of others showing themselves to me and at the same time
withdrawing from me, if I remain open to the very mystery of
God in them and in me, leads into an adventure that is an acceptance of love, it seems to me, an acceptance of life. I find serenity in the adventure itself.

I wonder sometimes, though, if I can tolerate so simple a life. "To accept life — but that is dangerous," H.D. says. "It is also dangerous not to accept life."[39] If I did not accept life, it would be because I could not endure the simplicity of letting be and living in openness to the mystery. It would be because of lack and loss in my life, because of suffering in the lives of others, because of the ways of God with human beings. It would be because of "the pain and despair of life." The danger of accepting life is having to suffer, to go through the pain and despair. The danger of not accepting is "to kill love," to become incapable of love, "to kill life," to become incapable of life. If I can bear so simple a life, accordingly, the serenity of letting be, the adventure of living in openness to the mystery, I do become capable of life and light and love.

"What gives us reason to go on living when we know what can happen to bring us back to our original solitude," Ralph Harper says, "is some demonstration that loneliness is not only relieved according to dearest and longest dreams, but may be transformed in ways beyond imagining."[40] When I lose someone who belongs to my life, I am brought back to my "original solitude." When I long for someone to make me unalone, I am caught up in "dearest and longest dreams." But when I embrace the simplicity of letting be and living in openness to the mystery, I let my loneliness "be transformed in ways beyond imagining." The transformation is in this, that my lack and my loss, my not having what others have, my not being what others are, is turned around into being what others are not, into knowing what others do not. I am a lonely man learning to love. I am like a blind man learning to see with his heart. If a human being's task in life is learning to love "with all your heart, and with all your soul, and with all your might,"[41] then mine is learning to love also with my sense of lack, and with my sense of loss.

It is learning to love with the longing in loneliness, a universal longing in my sense of lack, a particular longing for a particular person in my sense of loss. Say I give over all my longing to God, "Lord, all my longing is known to thee, my sighing is not hidden from thee."[42] There is letting be in this, and openness to the mystery. In letting be I am giving my longing over to God, counting on God to fulfill it. In being open to the mystery I am remaining open to the way in which God will fulfill it, whether with the presence of another human being, or even a reunion with the person I have lost, or with God's own presence in my life. My letting be, however, is not simply letting be, as Heidegger thinks of it, and openness to the mystery of Being, but letting be, as Meister Eckhart originally thought of it, and openness to the mystery of God.[43]

I am able to give my longing over to God but unable, I find, simply to let be, for giving it over to God is still longing, still caring. If I could simply let be, as Heidegger prescribes, without any reference to God, then I could say "Being is my desire." As it is, I want to say with Tolstoy, "God is my desire."[44] It is the difference between Something and Someone, between relating to Something and relating to Someone. It is true, thinking (*denken*) and thanking (*danken*) are one for Heidegger, and there is a hint of God in all he says of Being. "In the forest clearing to which his circular paths lead, though they do not reach it, Heidegger has postulated the unity of thought and of poetry," George Steiner says, "of thought, of poetry, and of the highest act of mortal pride and celebration which is to give thanks."[45] As for me, though, the paths of life lead to a clearing where we meet God. We find Being there, to be sure, in the shape of life and light and love, and we give thanks, but we find, as when we give our longing over to God, that thought and poetry and giving thanks come together in the act of prayer, in heart speaking to heart.

"God requires the heart," it is said in the Talmud, and likewise, I want to say, the heart requires God. It is in prayer that God's demand and the heart's demand do meet. The person I have to be and the person I want to be meet in the person I am meant to be, and that is the person I am before God, in the stance of prayer. The Talmudic saying occurs in a discussion of prayer, why some prayers are answered and others go unanswered, "But it is because the Holy One, blessed be He, requires the heart."[46] When I am heart and soul in my prayer, in my relationship with God, my prayer is answered. God requires wholeness, that is, but the heart requires God; requires participation, that is, to be caught up in life and light and love. There is a meeting of God and the heart thus, in which a human being comes *to be,* to exist to the utmost. All of life is there in prayer, I mean, as in the Psalms, the entire gamut of human feeling.

Is this not the end of desire, *a unity of thought and poetry, a unity of thinking and thanking, a unity of all life in prayer*? There is a formula in Paul's Epistle to the Philippians that leads us on from prayer to peace. "Have no anxiety about anything, but in everything by prayer and supplication with thanksgiving let your requests be made known to God," he says. "And the peace of God, which passes all understanding, will keep your minds and hearts in Christ Jesus."[47] So it is, the ending of desire is ultimately in *a peace that passes all understanding.* It is a peace we can taste already in this life in prayer, in contemplation, in thinking that is thanking. It is an eternal peace that "will keep your minds and hearts in Christ Jesus." Yet the formula is one of recurrence. I can feel the peace now whenever I turn my loneliness and my longing over to God, but I have to turn it over again and again. A wandering eye, a divided heart, a stifled cry, that is my repeated experience of unpeace, of restlessness. I have over and over to refocus my vision upon God, to reopen my heart to God, to cry out anew to God.

"An adequate life," Douglas Steere says, is "a life which has grasped intuitively the whole nature of things, and has seen and felt and refocused itself to this whole."[48] It is in grasping the unity of thought and poetry, of thinking and thanking, of all life in prayer, that I grasp intuitively "the whole nature of things," and it is in prayer, in turning over all my cares to God, that I see the light, that I feel the presence, that I refocus my life to the mystery of the whole. "Thinking is thanking" (*Denken ist Danken*), the mystic saying of the seventeenth century, is also a formula of recurrence. If I think back, calling things to mind, and if I thank God for them, one by one, I am "counting my blessings." Yet something profound is happening in me as I do it. I am coming into relation with all of my life, my joys and my sorrows, and even with all of life itself, its joys and its sorrows, and as I do so I am becoming whole, I am being healed of all my hurts.

A spiritual practice yields an experience that is recurrent but always incomplete. It is the turning of the wheel on a vehicle that is moving forward, the serenity of an adventure that is still going on. It is music meant to be repeatedly performed. A blind man I knew once wrote, after being very moved by music, "this was what I have been trying to do all my life . . . to reach out and create something the way music does . . . to express my sorrow." No, he decided, "that's not it," rather "to create seeing. . . . It is as though not seeing is a vacuum, and the fashioning of human bonds fills it up. It is as though that were light for me — and beauty." Or it is a matter, he said, "of being connected with the unknown, so that it can become known . . . there is beauty in connectedness with the unknown."[49] What he is describing, it seems to me, are stages of desire. For me, a lonely man learning to love, the stages are similar. First there is the desire to express my loneliness, then the desire to fill the void with human relations, and then at last the desire to find life and light and love in union or communion with God.

If the blind man gave no expression to his sorrow, if I gave none to my loneliness, we would go no further, unfeeling towards our own desire. If we did not seek to fill the void with human relations, we would never discover the deep longing that is still unconsummated in human intimacy. And if we did not follow the longing to connectedness with the unknown, to union or communion with God, we would never come to our heart's desire. As it is, we come to the serenity of an adventure into the unknown, the peace of a journey with God. We come to "the perpetual vision of the road which leads to the deeper realities."[50] For Whitehead those words describe "God in the world." For me they describe "God with us" (Emmanuel) or us with God, coming to share in the vision of God, insight by insight. The road is that of the heart's desire, and it leads to the deeper realities of knowing and of loving.

Learning to love seems to consist mainly in a subtle change

in orientation, from mimetic to heart's desire, from setting my heart on likeness to opening my heart to presence. I have to turn even from the imitation to the presence of Christ. I come then to likeness after all. It is like turning from the quest of certainty to the quest of understanding. I come then to certainty after all. It is like climbing the heights of Macchu Picchu. I was feeling heart's desire, feeling my heart rise there as I saw the sun rise. I was feeling peace of heart, sensing fulfillment, when I sat there at high noon, contemplating the beauty and the grandeur. And now I am feeling the contrast between mimetic and heart's desire, between trying to be like others in love and opening my heart to the love there is in my life. I come then to thought and to vision. I think on love and work, on rivalry in love, on rivalry in work. I can see violence arising from mimetic desire, nonviolence arising from heart's desire. I can see violent origins and peaceful ends; I can see the way from death to life.

2

Violent and Unviolent Ways

Such is the nature of force—those who use it and those who endure it are turned to stone.

—Simone Weil

Violence is said to come of desire; nonviolence of giving up desire; violence of zest for life, though it brings death; nonviolence of a sense that it is better not to be than to be, though it holds life sacred.[1] Heart's desire, I believe, is a clue here. Violence comes of unknowing desire, of "mimetic desire," as René Girard says, for violence itself is mimetic, with stroke and counterstroke, as in the feud of the Hatfields and McCoys. Nonviolence comes of giving up desire that is unknowing and unloving, for it comes of following the heart's desire to know and to love.

"I have chosen to learn what love is," Helen Luke says, "and therefore for a very long time I must give up doing what I will, that is, making unconscious compulsive choices, on the superficial level, in order to follow this deepest will in me to love, to be true to my individual way for which I am chosen, set apart."[2] It is only when I have passed from mimetic to heart's desire, it seems, when I am following "this deepest will in me to love," that I can take Augustine's words to heart, "Love and do what you will!"[3] Before I come to that I am doing what I see others doing, choosing what I see others choosing. I am miming them, even miming myself at an earlier stage, following urges I once had, desires I once entertained, without regard to my deepest longings. "I don't think I was desiring what others desire," a friend wrote to me, "so much as desiring what I'd seen myself desire in the past." To go beyond the past I make a commitment to my unknown heart's desire, to learn to love, "I have chosen to learn what love is," and from choosing I come to a sense of being chosen and to the sense of a way that is truly mine.

22

I come to an unviolent way, it seems, if and only if I have chosen to learn what love is. Otherwise I may come to a violent way, I may be driven, that is, to violence. It is true, there is still another alternative, to have no way at all. For even a violent way is a way, is *War Music*,[4] as Christopher Logue calls its poetry, a music of war that gives form and direction to the chaotic passions of violence. I think of Gandhi's insight into what he called "a Himalayan miscalculation,"[5] into his initial mistake of thinking a mass of people is capable not only of violence but also of nonviolence. When peaceful demonstrations he organized turned into riots, it became clear to him that peaceful action, like warlike action, is not possible without a spiritual discipline, a music of peace like the music of war, a learning to love that leads to a seeing of truth. "To see the universal and all-pervading Spirit of Truth face to face," he says, "one must be able to love the meanest of creation as oneself."[6]

Is it true then, as Gandhi originally thought, "The people are not by nature violent but peaceful"?[7] To me it seems we become violent by following mimetic desire, peaceful by following our heart's desire. Do we come of violent beginnings, as René Girard argues, and are we headed for violent ends? I think again of the old man of the desert and his words to T. E. Lawrence, "The love is from God and of God and towards God,"[8] as if to say our heart's desire has its beginning and its end in God. Let us consider our ways, where they come from and where they are leading. We carry imagination to its limits when we imagine origins and ends. Let us see what happens if we try to imagine the unimaginable.

Violent Origins

"The present type of order in the world has arisen from an unimaginable past," A. N. Whitehead says, "and it will find its grave in an unimaginable future."[9] He is speaking of the order of the universe, and yet he is speaking of the world for us, our world, what we can imagine and what is beyond our imagination. If the origin and the end of our world is unimaginable, it is because our world is all we know from experience. When we imagine the unimaginable, when we tell the story of our world, its origin and its end, we are engaged in mythmaking. There is a profound link, nevertheless, between myth and the basic human story, the story of a life from birth to death. My life too has arisen from an unimaginable past, unimaginable to me because in it I do not yet exist and my existence, the fact that I am, is the core of my experience. My life too will find its grave in an unimaginable future, unimaginable to me because in it I will exist in a way I do not yet exist now or in a way I do exist now but only on the deepest levels of my consciousness of knowing and of loving.

So human society as we know it has arisen, I see too, from an unimaginable past and will find its grave in an unimaginable future. If we tell a story of its origins, if we speak of a founding murder as Augustine did, comparing Romulus and Remus to Cain and Abel, or as Girard has done in our time, imagining a lynch mob turning into a society by way of the unanimous violence of killing a scapegoat,[10] we are trying to imagine the unimaginable past, we are engaged in mythmaking. Still, there may be a profound link between the myth and the violence of the human story we do know. It may be that human society, like human purpose, as Shakespeare has it, is "of violent birth, but poor validity."[11] The real question of violent origins is the origin of our violence. Where does it come from?

Imagining the unimaginable is imaging the unknown. Although the unknown is unknown, I do know of the unknown, and that is how I come to image it. *What do I know of the unknown?* Much of what I know is in the insight that violence is mimetic, doing unto others as they do unto you, that it arises from mimetic desire, wanting what others want, I would say from unknowing desire, not knowing what you want. "I reserve the word desire for what happens to appetites and needs when they become contaminated with imitation or even entirely displaced by it," Girard says. "Man is the creature who does not know what to desire, and he turns to others in order to make up his mind."[12] For Girard, then, desire has no content of its own. For me there is the heart's desire, our desire to know and be known, to love and be loved, ultimately our desire for God, in whom we find the fullness of knowing and of loving. The heart's desire does not begin by knowing what it desires, I believe, and so it looks to others to learn. Mimetic desire, for me therefore, is simply the heart's desire before it knows what it wants. The unknown is an unknowing.

If I go back in thought to my own beginning, thinking back through my own memories, I come back also, as Augustine found in his *Confessions,* to the beginning of the world, as if my own origins were simultaneous with the origins of my world, as if the beginning of a life were contemporary somehow with the very beginning of time. I come back, as Girard finds in his reading of the Gospels, to "things hidden since the foundation of the world."[13] Let me see how far I can go, if I can come not only to an image of the unknown but to an insight into the image, if in coming into touch with heart's desire I can pass from unknowing to knowing.

Searching for God in time and memory, Augustine found God by going to the limit of memory, to the beginning beyond which there is a personal nothingness, no "I am." He found God in time only by going to the edge of time, in memory only by going to the edge of memory. Here is the paradox I come upon in thinking back to the unknown. "But the image has touched the depths," as Gaston Bachelard says, "before it stirs the surface."[14] The unknown has touched the depths of the heart before it stirs the surface of memory. God has lived in me as my heart's desire before I come to know of God. So learning is remembering, even here, not so much remembering something I have already known as remembering something I have already desired and have known only in the unknowing of desiring. I desire happiness, but don't realize it is to be found in God alone. I desire to know and be known, to love and be loved, but don't realize I desire God until I actually taste the knowing and the loving that come of God. So God is in my desire and desire is in my memory, but memory alone is not enough without understanding and will.

And because desire is unknowing, even unwilling, a kind of groping and stumbling, it can become violent, attacking and fleeing and collapsing. "Where then did I find Thee, that I might learn Thee? For in my memory Thou were not, before I learned Thee," Augustine exclaimed. "Where then did I find Thee, that I might learn Thee, but in Thee above me?"[15] There is an illumining that comes from "above me," according to this, a tasting of the knowing and the loving that come of God, an illumining of desire, I want to say, in which desire becomes knowing and willing, and it makes the difference, I want to say too, between violent and unviolent ways. It comes from "above me" because desire as in me, as in my memory, is unknowing and unwilling. Life and light and love must come from "above me," therefore, to change me from unknowing to knowing, from unwilling to willing, from violent to peaceable.

As I think back, though, I can see how "the image has touched the depths before it stirs the surface." God has been at work in my life at unawares, without my knowing, without my willing, in things happening, hap and mishap, happiness and unhappiness, in my fleeing from unhappiness, even from life as full of unhappiness, from what was supposed to be "fun" but was really unhappy, in my seeking for happiness — I remember looking at faces, going from face to face, looking for someone who was happy, someone from whom I could learn the secret of happiness. God was there somehow in the things I did to master life, to discover the secret, using the magic of words, giving expression to my hopes and fears, hoping to realize my hopes, to overcome my fears, my fear of death, my fear of love. If magic is knowing the true names of things, then I found magic indeed in being able to name my hopes and fears, even to name my heart's desire. It is in naming my heart's desire, as I am doing now, that I come to name God.

It is here too, in naming my heart's desire, that I come to the parting of the ways, of violent and unviolent ways, for if I leave out some place in my heart, if I ignore some inner voice in naming it, that part of me will despair and become desperate and may turn to violence. Even if I say "God is my desire," I may mean I desire to be God and want to follow "the appeal of mastery," as Karen Horney calls it, or I may mean I desire to have God and want to follow "the appeal of love," or I may mean my desire itself is God living in me and I want to follow "the appeal of freedom."[16] If I leave out love, for the sake of freedom or mastery, I will despair and become desperate, and so too if I leave out mastery or freedom. It is only if God is all in all to me, only if all these things exist in God for me, that I can say "God is my desire" without doing violence to myself and provoking myself to violence.

Naming is "originally an act of violence that discloses being,"[17] Martin Heidegger says, and so it is, or can be with naming hopes and fears, and especially with naming heart's desire. In her earlier work Karen Horney had spoken of "moving against people" instead of "mastery," of "moving toward people" instead of "love" and of "moving away from people" instead of "freedom." She named these aspects of heart's desire in terms of human relations, that is, and only later in terms of selfhood. I am proposing to go one step further by naming them in terms of God. At every point, nevertheless, there is "an act of violence that discloses being." It discloses first our relations with one another, then at the heart of these our relations with ourselves, and then at the heart of these our relations with God. Neurosis occurs, according to Horney, when any of the aspects becomes compulsive, when it becomes separate and exclusive of the others. The violence of naming is in the separation and exclusion. Heidegger tries to overcome the exclusion by using the most inclusive name, Being, but he comes then, as he says, to "violent gathering."

"In the beginning was the Word," the opening words of the Gospel of John, suggest neither a violent separation nor a violent gathering but a beginning in life and light and love. There is an unviolent way of naming, it seems from this, a way of naming our hopes and fears, of naming our heart's desire, that neither separates us in our loneliness, moving against one another, moving toward one another, moving away from one another, nor gathers us in an unanimity of violence to achieve mastery or love or freedom, but opens us instead to life and light and love. Instead of moving against, moving toward, moving away, I let heart speak to heart ("Heart speaks to heart"). Instead of forestalling my heart by pursuing mastery or love or freedom, I let my heart speak ("My heart speaks clearly at last").[18] Instead of naming God, I let God be unknown and become known to me, I let the Word speak to my heart.

"In the beginning was the deed," the substitution that takes place in Goethe's *Faust,* goes with the feeling "It's impossible to put such trust in the Word."[19] The deed here hints of violence, of violent origins, of Cain killing Abel to found the first city, of Romulus killing Remus to found Rome. Maybe this is the origin after all of violence. If I cannot put such trust in the Word, if I cannot take the Word to heart, then the deed becomes the only expression of my heart's desire, but without the Word it is an expression that is unknowing, that is unloving. I think of "the most decisive acts of life," as Reiner Schürmann calls them, "the foundation of a family or of a community," "a dialogue that actualizes 'two words of existence,'" "the acceptance of destiny."[20] If I am letting the Word speak to my heart, then the foundation is without violence, the dialogue is of heart to heart, the acceptance is with hope, but if I cannot put such trust in the Word, the foundation has to be secured with force, the dialogue partakes of the violence of naming, the acceptance has to be without hope.

I think of the violence I feel when I take action, when I decide to go on a journey, for instance, simply out of restlessness and not with any sense of being called or being led. It is the same restlessness of desire that undermines words of promise such as those of the marriage covenant, "I take you . . . to have and to hold . . . for better, for worse . . . until death do us part," or does not allow them to stand without words also of forgiveness. All the decisive acts of life are there, the foundation of a family, a dialogue of "two words of existence," an acceptance of destiny. Those two words must become words not only of promise but also of forgiveness, though, and even then "It's impossible to put such trust in the Word" unless the restlessness of desire can somehow be stayed, unless we can find rest somehow in restlessness, unless the Word illumines desire somehow and brings it to rest.

An illumining of desire does come about, it seems, when we realize we are "words of existence," when we let the Word speak to our hearts, I mean, and let it reveal to us the truth of our lives, and come to realize we ourselves then have a truth to reveal to others. Sometimes we feel driven to search for the truth of our lives, to know the truth about ourselves, to know the worst — "she had to walk the path she had chosen to the end, for the sake of her choice, for the sake of her pride, for her own sake," Friedrich Dürrenmatt tells in a novel, "a ridiculous and nevertheless implacable vicious circle of duty, but it was the truth she was seeking, the truth about herself."[21] To know the worst can mean to know our desire to die, to know our desire to live, to live at all costs, to see others die in our stead. It can mean to know our inner violence. The truth that comes to light in knowing the worst, though, is only a corruption, "the corruption of the best is the worst" (*corruptio optimi pessima*). The truth that is revealed by the Word speaking to the heart, on the other hand, is not just the worst, not just the corruption, but the best. The illumining of desire is in knowing the best, not in knowing the worst, for it is in knowing the best of me that I come to a sense of being called, of being led.

What is the difference between the best and the worst in me, between being led by the best and being driven by the worst? It is the difference between rest and restlessness. Yet this is not a gross difference, for I find rest in restlessness, quiet in unquiet. Before I come to rest I feel only emptiness and insecurity when I contemplate the future, as in Kierkegaard's parable of the falling spider, placed at the beginning and in the middle of Dürrenmatt's story:

> What will come? What will the future bring? I do not know. I have no presentiment. When a spider plunges from a fixed point to its consequences, it always sees before it an empty space where it can never set foot, no matter how it wriggles. It is that way

with me: before me always an empty space; what drives me forward is a consequence that lies behind me. This life is perverse and frightful, it is unbearable.[22]

From being driven to being led, that is the inner change that takes place in me, as I feel it, when I consent to restlessness and find rest, so subtle a change that it can seem no change at all. And yet I do change from being driven by "a consequence that lies behind me" to being led by a light that goes before me.

It is "a consequence" or, according to another translation, "a consistency" that lies behind me, that drives me forward as long as I am prey to restless desire. Thus "life is perverse" or, according to another translation, "topsy-turvy" or, according to another, "backward." This consequence or consistency is a change of causation, like karma, like the pendulum motion of violence and counterviolence, the consequence or consistency of mimetic desire, of mirrors reflecting one another. It is broken by the word of promise, looking to the future, by the word of forgiveness, looking to the past, by the Word that was in the beginning, revealed as promise in the Old Testament, as forgiveness in the New. Instead of the future reaching into the present and shaping it as if the future were a past, the consequence, the consistency behind me, I become free of the past and open to the future by putting trust in the Word. I am led then by the kindly light of promise and forgiveness, a light that transfigures the past and the future, a light that gives me thereby the present.

Here is the illumining that comes from "above me," freeing me from the consequence that comes from "behind me." There is a kind of rest in movement, a serenity in adventure, in the sense of being led rather than being driven or simply wandering. It is true, I am not relieved of the future consequences of my acts in the past. Still, my relationship with them changes and so their significance also changes. As Hannah Arendt says, the consequences of our acts multiply beyond our knowing and beyond our control. Our relationship with them is changed, though, by forgiveness and by promise, by "the power of forgiveness," as she says, and "the power of promise."[23] No doubt, it is we who forgive and we who promise. It is by putting trust in the Word, though, that I open myself to the power of promise and forgiveness. It is God, then, who promises, God who forgives, when I stand thus to the past and the future; God who leads.

"I trembled with love and awe," Augustine says, describing this illumining, "and I perceived myself to be far off from Thee, in the region of unlikeness."[24] I come to know my distance, my unlikeness, but in the light of my longing for intimacy with God. If I were to know only the distance, only the unlikeness, it would be by observing and being observed, as in Dürrenmatt's story, "On the Observing of the Observer of the Observers," as he calls it, for in observing and being observed I keep my distance. I see myself living and I see myself dying, I observe thus my desire to live and my desire to die, but I do not feel my desire as a longing for union with God unless I enter into it, unless I dwell in it, learning to love with all my heart and with all my soul and with all my might. If I do enter in, embracing the truth of my life in the trust of forgiveness and promise, I can still observe myself from the midst of indwelling, see myself distant from God while longing for God. I see the distance, though, because I feel it. It is only "in the region of unlikeness," I can see, that there is "an unimaginable past" and "an unimaginable future."

It is the story that decides what can be told of the past and the future, I can see, much as in physics, as Einstein said to Heisenberg, "it is the theory which decides what can be observed."[25] I am caught up in a story, I mean, in the consequences of acts that lie behind me. Being in the story, I do not know how it will end, whether it will have a happy or a sad ending. Likewise I do not know how it began, in thought or word or deed, for the thread of my life is woven in with that of others, and when I think back, just as when I think forward, I come to a darkness of unknowing. Being also a teller of the story, nevertheless, I can choose to live toward one ending rather than another, toward eternal life rather than death, and I can choose to live out of one beginning rather than another. I have a choice, that is, whether the story shall begin "In the beginning was the Word" or "In the beginning was the deed."

Not that there is no true story, but the true story comes to light when I enter fully into the story, giving my heart to my life, embracing my heart's desire. If I remain an observer, entering into the story only by being observed, then God too seems only an observer, for "only if God were a pure observer could he remain unsullied by his creation," and the difference between us and God would be that we not only observe but are observed — "God was not subject to observation, God's freedom consisted in being a concealed, hidden god, while man's bondage consisted of being observed."[26] There is something more basic than observation, though, if "it is the theory which decides what can be observed," namely the choice that sets up the theory, the choice of either giving or withholding my heart. That is Kierkegaard's own answer to his parable of the falling spider, the "Either/Or" of our choice. If I do choose to give my heart, if I do choose to put such trust in the Word of forgiveness and of promise, then the violence of the human story becomes for me a darkness in which the light shines ("The light shines in the darkness . . .").

Violence then goes with the alternative, to withhold my heart, to find it impossible to put such trust in the word ("and the darkness did not comprehend it" or "has not overcome it"). As Tolkien says, "whereas the light perceives the very heart of the darkness, its own secret has not been discovered."[27] The choice, in Augustine's terms, is whether to belong only to the human city or to the more encompassing city of God, or in mine, to look back only to violent origins or to origins in life and light and love, to look forward only to death or to eternal life. As I am conceiving it, the choice has to do with our relationship to the past and the future more than with the simple facts. There is violence in the human past and maybe also in the human future, but I can choose to look beyond violence, exercising the power of forgiveness and of promise, to let life and light and love flow into the present.

Purpose and Cross-Purpose

If the heart's desire is dark on the violent way and luminous on the unviolent way, it may be because force is numbing

to the heart, because "those who use it and those who endure
it," as Simone Weil says, "are turned to stone."[28] Yet one may
end up having to endure it even if one walks the unviolent way.
What then? "Grace can prevent this touch from corrupting him,"
she says, "but it cannot spare him the wound."[29] As I say these
things, I realize I am changing the subject from the cause to the
effect of violence. Unless the effect is again the cause, unless
violence arises from a numbness of heart which is itself due to
violence. And so it seems to be. We do unto others as they do
unto us, or more accurately, as has been done already unto us,
receiving violence from some and giving it in our turn to others,
the abused becoming the abusers. Violence thus is mimetic, violence breeding violence, and its cause beyond violence itself is
mimetic desire. And so there is the conflict of violent purposes
with one another, but the essential conflict is that of violent and
unviolent purposes, of mimetic and heart's desire.

Considering only violent purposes, I could see the conflict
of purpose and cross-purpose issuing into an outcome like the
resultant of vectors of force in physics, something intended by
neither, an outcome that might be simply a mutual destruction,
not necessarily "the cunning of reason,"[30] as Hegel called it, as
if it were a higher or more subtle purpose. Still, there is a higher
or more subtle purpose at work, I do believe, the heart's desire
working even through mimetic desires, "the demonic element"
as Goethe called it, "which is in the play on both sides, in the
conflict of which the lovely goes under and the hated triumphs,
and then the prospect that out of this a third will spring, which
will correspond to the wish of all."[31] If it does indeed "correspond
to the wish of all," if it corresponds, I mean, to the deepest longings of the human heart, it may be seen as heart's desire. Yet
what is it?

It must be something beyond the conflict of opposing causes,
of party with party—not just another cause but something hu-
manly complete, something whole and entire like the human being. It must be the person, the whole we each are, or the common good, the whole that is greater than ourselves. "When I
despair, I remember that all through history the way of truth
and love has always won," Gandhi said to Mirabehn. "There have

been tyrants and murderers, and for a time they can seem invincible. But in the end they always fall." He said that to encourage her. "Think of it — always . . .," he told her. "When you are in doubt that that is God's way, the way the world is meant to be . . . think of that."[32] If he is right, then it holds true even in the apparent defeat of goodness, as in his own assassination. Here there is the person in that of Gandhi himself, and there is the common good in "the way of truth and love." The person emerges even in death and defeat, and the common good is realized, "the way of truth and love" is opened up for everyone.

Is it really the common good, though, that emerges on the unviolent way or is it only the person who walks on this way? It has been argued that the unviolent way is really the pursuit of "personal holiness, at the expense of public good."[33] Nonviolence is indeed a way of life, I want to say, not just a technique for resolving conflict. As a way of life it is essential to personal holiness but also to public good. It embodies the higher and more universal purpose in the conflict of purpose and cross-purpose.

What is a purpose? "The aim to live in a certain way — not to quiver with feelings," A. T. Wright answers in his novel *Islandia.* "Aims come before you are conscious of them. They are not wholly thoughts originating in your mind."[34] Consider *Satyagraha,* the opera by Philip Glass about Gandhi in South Africa, the libretto taken entirely from verses of the Gita that guided Gandhi in life, and the three acts named for his forerunner Tolstoy, his contemporary Tagore, and his successor King. The verses suggest the higher and more universal purpose, but the setting in South Africa and the scenes suggest the conflict in Gandhi's time and also in our own time. It was in South Africa that purpose emerged for Gandhi, before he was conscious of it, and not wholly as a thought originating in his mind, but he found a name for it, a combination of Satya (truth), "the aim to live in a certain way," we could say, and Agraha (firmness), "not to quiver with feelings." I can feel the force of it when I am quivering with feelings, restless, my heart divided, my eye wandering, or feeling let down, nursing a grudge, a stifled cry. There is strength in purpose, in living in a certain way, just as there is weakness in quivering with feelings.

Still, there is feeling in purpose, an intensity of feeling that comes of simplicity or a simplicity that comes of intensity. "The aim to live in a certain way" in Wright's novel as in the Gita is the aim to live in an unselfish way, to live without ulterior motive. So the purpose is indeed "to live in a certain way" and not, rather, to gain pleasure or profit or victory. The words of the Gita ring out again and again in the opera, "Hold pleasure and pain, profit and loss, victory and defeat to be the same: then brace yourself for the fight. So will you bring no evil on yourself."[35] It is not that you are to have no feeling about pleasure and pain, profit and loss, victory and defeat, but that your heart is to be, rather, in the way of life. Instead of "detachment" I prefer to use the word "heart-free," because there is "heart" in "heart-free"; there is heart in the living, in being heart-free toward the gaining and the losing.

If the conflict is one of ways, as the conflict in South Africa was seen to be, of Eastern and Western ways of life, of migrant workers from India led by the young Gandhi and Western colonials led by General Jan Smuts, it can be resolved only by a purification of ways through renunciation of pleasure and profit and victory, or so Gandhi thought, only by overcoming the fear of pain and loss and defeat. There is a simplicity, an intensity, that comes of going to the heart of the matter, to the heart of a way, of going from mimetic or competitive desire to heart's desire. The words of the Gita resounding over the Eastern way are like the words of the Sermon on the Mount would be resounding over the Western way, a call to purity of heart, to willing one thing. By going to the heart of the matter, we come to a convergence of ways, I mean, a concord of wills. But what if the seeking of pleasure, of profit, of victory were the essence of the way? Then renunciation would mean renunciation of the way itself. It would mean this way of life was a path without a heart. For if it is a path of heart, it will survive the fire of simplicity and intensity.

How do we get to the heart of the matter? By "heart-searching," by discovering "the particular way," by "resolution" to follow it, Martin Buber says in *The Way of Man*.[36] Thus in the first act of the opera the first scene, "The Kuru Field of Justice," transposes the situation of the Gita into that of Gandhi in South Africa; the second scene, "Tolstoy Farm," depicts the simple way of life Gandhi and his followers embrace; and the third scene, "The Vow," shows them bracing themselves for the struggle against racial prejudice. Heart-searching is like an encounter with death, it seems to me, when you realize you are going to die someday and see, in that light, what matters and what doesn't matter. As the many things that do not matter drop away, a way of life emerges that is simpler than the way you were following, simpler and more intense. Resolving upon the way means accepting death, then, in advance, resolving to live as if all that mattered were what matters in the light of death.

Accepting death in advance, being willing to die rather than to kill, seems to be the essence of Satyagraha. I think of the story of the Zen master who overcame the fear of death. A master swordsman was asked to train the bodyguards of a ruler. Interviewing them, he came upon one who seemed to have the air of a master. "You are already a master," he said to him. "No," he replied. "Haven't you mastered something?" the swordsman insisted. "No," he replied again, "the only thing I can think of is that once I was very afraid of death and now I no longer live in fear." "If you have mastered the fear of death," the swordsman said, "then you are indeed a master."[37] So there is a mastery in this, something like a Zen mastery, in overcoming the fear of death. It is done by accepting death, however, not by convincing oneself that one's fear is groundless. Thus too it does not mean feeling no fear so much as being able to live with the feeling on account of one's willingness to die. It is a peace that comes of making peace with death itself. It is a Yes to death as part of life and thus really a full Yes to life.

There is something of the way of the warrior in this, there is "war music" in it — I think of the well-known photo of the young Gandhi as a Satyagrahi. Still, it is a way even for those who are unable to defend themselves. The first scene of act 2 of the opera shows Gandhi meeting an angry mob on his return from India to South Africa and being rescued by Mrs. Alexander, the wife of the constable, and escaping under the symbolic protection of her parasol. There is willingness to die here in meeting the mob, there is hope to live, nevertheless, in the fleeing, and there is something very universal in the combination, willingness and hope, a way even for the defenseless, a strength, a courage to be, even for the weak and the unarmed. "Though action rages without, the heart can be tuned to produce unbroken music."[38] The tuning of the heart is by willingness and by hope, the music is of peace.

"None of its notes is final," Tagore says, "yet each reflects the infinite."[39] If I myself live in peace, if I live in willingness and hope, I live from moment to moment, and yet each passing moment reflects eternal peace, each reflects a reality that is greater than myself. "To begin with oneself," Buber says in *The Way of Man,* and yet "not to be preoccupied with oneself."[40] The second scene of act 2 of the opera shows Gandhi and his followers beginning with themselves, working on the newspaper *Indian Opinion,* which was first of all a critical reflection on themselves, but moving on to reflect also on the larger society in which they were living. "None of its notes is final," for the reflection is upon a way, upon a conflict of ways, upon a possible convergence of ways, yet like the words of the Gita "each reflects the infinite," because of dropping all that does not matter for those who are going to die, because of being willing to die and yet hoping to live, because of believing it is possible to live in peace.

"Here where one stands,"[41] Buber says in *The Way of Man,* is where one finds the treasure of the heart's desire. It is possible to live in peace where one is, Gandhi thought, to take one's stand there, whether one is a native or a colonial or a migrant. To live in peace is to "feel hatred for no being," he sings in the opera, to "be friendly, compassionate."[42] It is to begin with oneself, eliminating all hatred from one's own heart, but not to stop with oneself. It is to live in an undivided house, as would be said now in the days of the struggle against *apartheid.* Thus the third scene of act 2 shows Gandhi and his followers burning their registration cards to protest the Black Act, which required all migrants from India to register and allowed police to enter their houses to inspect their certificates. The words of the Gita are sung again,

"Hold pleasure and pain, profit and loss, victory and defeat to be the same. . . ."

It is possible to live in peace, according to this, even in a "time of troubles." It is possible if you have already accepted death in advance. For the troubles of the time of troubles, war and famine and plague and death, the Four Horsemen of the Apocalypse, all are shapes of death. To live in peace is easier in some times, when death is not such a present reality, and harder in others. I think of a friend of mine who says "We must learn to live in peace now in the present, when it is easier, so we will be able to live in it then in the future, when it will be harder." I can see, nevertheless, that the basic difficulty is the same, now and then, the acceptance of death. "This is the fixed, still state which sustains even at the time of death the athletes of the spirit," Gandhi and his followers sing from the Gita, "who even then set forth, some to return, some never to return."[43] They sing this in the last act of the opera, which shows the Satyagraha army slowly entering, singing, while Gandhi reviews them, and contemporary police also entering and slowly escorting the army offstage, several at a time. This "fixed, still state" which allows them to accept arrest is their peace with death.

"Some to return, some never to return" suggests hope and the future. This last act ends with Gandhi looking upwards to the level above, where he sees Martin Luther King and sees the Satyagraha army reappear behind King in silence and then fade out. He is looking into the future, that is, with eyes of hope. It is as if he himself were to return in King and as if his followers were to return in King's followers. Death, though accepted, is not the end. Gandhi's last words in the opera are those of Krishna in the Gita, "I come into being age after age and take a visible shape and move a man with men for the protection of good, thrusting the evil back and setting virtue on her seat again."[44] God takes human form in every age, he is saying, moving among us, a human being among human beings, working for good, working against evil. God comes again, Gandhi did actually believe, in every one of us.

God in us is the common good. Personal holiness is only

a transparency that allows God to shine through. Some persons are opaque; some are translucent; some are transparent. There is a way, though, that leads from opaque to transparent. It is that of "reducing oneself to zero," according to Gandhi, that of "submitting one's will to God," according to his Muslim follower, Badshah Khan, that of "courageous self-affirmation,"[45] according to his Christian follower, Martin Luther King. Yet the reducing of oneself to nothing is before God dwelling within one, the submission of will is to that of God guiding one, the courageous self-affirmation is simply receiving oneself from the hand of God. By relating to myself and willing to be myself, I am "grounded transparently" in God.[46] All of these ways lead to the same place, transparency towards God, the presence of God in us. The common good is in each and every person. That is always the issue in nonviolent struggles, it seems, the recognition of an outcast people as human beings, of the "untouchables" in India, for example, as *harijan* or "children of God."

Where the difference comes between religions is in the acceptance of death, accepting it because God's light in me lives and shines on even after my death, or accepting it because my individuality itself lives on as a unique refraction of God's light. If God becomes incarnate in every age, as in the Gita, even in every person, as for Gandhi, it is God in us who lives on. If there is a unique incarnation in Jesus, the Christian belief, there is more to our uniqueness, our individuality; the "I am" of Jesus brings to light the "I am" of everyone else. If there is no incarnation, as in Islam, then we are all human beings, nevertheless, before God. It is God who lives on, according to all, and we live insofar as we have to do with God. If there were no God, no one who lives on, nothing that lasts, it would be possible still to accept death but not to accept it with hope.

"A great desire is thought to be a universal one,"[47] Gaston Bachelard says. If there is, as I believe, a heart's desire, there is a universal principle capable of resolving every conflict of purpose and cross-purpose, every conflict of ways, every conflict even of religions. The resolution of conflict seems to depend, however, on a combination of willingness and hope, a willingness to die and a hope to live. That is what Gandhi and Khan and King, coming from Hinduism and Islam and Christianity, seem to have shared, a willingness and a hope. Each one of them could have said with Tolstoy, "God is my desire." If we go further afield and consider also Buddhism, we find the willingness to die but without the hope, without desire, without any God. Instead there is a reverence for life, a compassion for all living beings. Perhaps that reverence and compassion converge with what I am calling "hope" and "heart's desire," especially if we think of the human heart as restless until it rest in God, for hope and desire are moving then toward a peace with everyone and everything.

It is the peace that is universal, desired by all, affirmed even in the renunciation of all desire. It still makes a difference, though, it seems to me, how we come to peace, whether by renouncing all that is against it or by following our heart's desire. "We will more and more often find ourselves faced with an implacable necessity," Girard says. "The definitive renunciation of violence, without any second thoughts, will become for us the condition *sine qua non* for the survival of humanity itself and for each one of us."[48] We may be forced to renounce all that is opposed to peace, he is saying, all violence, all mimetic desire, simply for the sake of survival. I can hope nevertheless that if we come to it this way, by necessity more than by choice, by choosing necessity, I should say, we will come to realize it is the peace of God, the fulfillment of heart's desire.

"Dancing Madly Backwards," the name of a variety store that once existed somewhere in New England, is a good name for such a "journey into God."[49] It is as if we were to back into peace, to back into the arms of God. Here is "the cunning of reason" in its true form. The direction we are looking is that of our purpose, but there is also the direction we are not looking. It is as if one were moving forwards when one is practicing nonviolence and backwards when one is on the other end of nonviolence. I know the experience of being on the other end of it, an experience that has been described by those who had to deal with Gandhi, some of whom, like Smuts, became his friends. I remember in childhood the experience of being met with nonviolence, a boy with whom I argued and came to blows but who would not return my blows. There is a surprise and a bewilderment. You don't know what to do. You do indeed find yourself "dancing madly backwards." You are moving in a direction you have not been looking. You were expecting to be moving forwards in the direction of your purpose, but you find yourself moving backwards in the direction of another purpose, as if you were fighting against God.

"No one against God but God," Goethe says, quoting a proverb, *Nemo contra Deum nisi Deus ipse.*[50] Even Satan, whose name means "enemy," is conceived in the Book of Job not as the enemy of God but of the human race. In conflicts of purpose and cross-purpose, of ways, of religions, nothing can be set against God but God. The unity of God seems then the fundamental resolution of human conflict. It is the opposing notions of God that are set against one another, the ways of life, the purposes and cross-purposes they involve. Goethe was thinking of the "daimonic man" who can be defeated by no human adversary but only by the universe itself, like Napoleon in Russia, but I am thinking with Tolstoy in *War and Peace* that Napoleon was "dancing madly backwards" in Russia from a people who did not accept defeat in battle as defeat. The unity of God is stronger than our notions of God, the peace of God stronger than our war.

Peaceful Ends

If you do not accept defeat in battle as defeat, then ultimately you do not accept force as the final argument in human affairs. That seems to have been the logic of Tolstoy's long journey from *War and Peace,* where he studied violence, to *The Kingdom of God Is Within You,* where he embraced nonviolence. Indeed if the unity of God is stronger than our notions of God, the peace of God stronger than our war, there is hope of perpetual peace. It is true, there is an irony in that phrase. Kant saw a Dutch innkeeper's sign where the words "perpetual peace"[51] were inscribed over the image of a graveyard. There is a kind of religious thinking, an apocalyptic faith, that looks forward to war, to an ultimate struggle of good and evil, to a final destruction of the world. I have learned, to my surprise, that the roots of apocalyptic faith are nonviolent, "the apocalyptic literature, all of it, has its setting in that part of the nation subscribing to nonviolent conduct."[52] The fundamental question here, I think, is "What kind of story are we in?" Are we in a story that ends in the peace of concord or one that ends in the peace of death?

It may be of the essence of the story that, being in it, we do not know how it ends. "I wonder what sort of a tale we've fallen into?" Sam asks in Tolkien's story, *The Lord of the Rings*. "I wonder. But I don't know," Frodo answers. "And that's the way of a real tale. Take any one you're fond of. You may know, or guess, what kind of a tale it is, happy-ending or sad-ending, but the people in it don't know. And you don't want them to."[53] There are actually two answers here. One is "You may know. . . ." The other is "the people in it don't know. . . ." As one who hears the story told, you may know. As one who is in the story, though, you don't know. If you try to combine the two perspectives and live in a story that you already know or have heard, the story changes to accommodate you, and the ending, instead of matching your expectations, comes as a surprise. Yet this very change may fulfill prophecy.

Take "The Immortal Story"[54] by Isak Dinesen. It is the story of a story, of a sailor's tale about a sailor who is hired by a rich old man to sleep a night with his young but childless wife. Here is how it goes. An old merchant, who spends his sleepless nights listening to his accounts being read by a clerk, asks the clerk to read him some other kind of account. The clerk, who is a wandering Jew, reads a chapter from Isaiah the prophet that he carries about with him on a slip of paper. The rich old man is bewildered by this prophecy which seems to promise an end to his own troubles. He hates anything that is not simple fact. It is then that he remembers the sailor's tale. When the clerk tells him the sailor's tale too is only a tale and not a fact, the old man determines to make it come true. He has the clerk find a young woman, and he himself hires the sailor. All seems to go as in the tale. But the old man dies during the night, and thus the prophecy is fulfilled that promises an end of his troubles, "and sorrow and sighing shall flee away."[55] The woman sees his death as revenge for her father, whom the old man years before had driven to suicide. And the sailor sees no likeness between the sailor's tale and what really happened between him and the woman, and has no intention of telling the tale of himself.

According to the story, I gather, the word becomes flesh, not matter of fact. It becomes flesh and blood human beings, I mean, not simply something that is so. "The secret of Truth is as follows," João Ubaldo Ribeiro says, "there are no facts, there are only stories."[56] That saying of his is itself the epigraph of a story he tells. The truth, I want to say, is really the word made flesh, human beings of flesh and blood. It is here, where flesh meets word, that the two worlds meet, this world and the other world whose presence is felt in this world, whose revelation takes place in this world. Apocalyptic faith, if we examine it according to word and flesh, is not a matter of fact but of passionate hope.

"Do you mean this world or is there another?" Violaine is asked in Paul Claudel's *Tidings Brought to Mary*. "There are two," she replies, "but I say there is only one and that is enough."[57] This world and the other world, she is saying, are really one world, and so anything can happen, miracles can happen. It is a world of passionate hope rather than of simple facts. The opposite point of view is what Miguel de Unamuno calls "the tragic sense of life,"[58] where neither world can be fully accepted, where imagination and reality are set off sharply against one another, this world linked with reality, the other with imagination, and we are left like Don Quixote, dissatisfied with the world of facts but unable to live in the world of stories. Our only way out is, like Don Quixote on his deathbed, to accept this world where life ends in death and yet be open to the mystery of the other world where life goes on after death. Acceptance, letting be and openness to mystery, leads into a vision where the two worlds are really one and one world is enough, a sense of truth that is more than facts, more even than stories.

"I say there is only one and that is enough," Violaine says, "and the mercy of God is boundless," she adds. This, I want to say, is the true essence of apocalyptic faith. It is to believe

(a) this world and the other world are one;

(b) the one world is enough; and

(c) the mercy of God is boundless.

I think of the Book of Jonah, though it is not a piece of apocalyptic literature, for in it there is a prophetic warning that the city will be destroyed, and yet the destruction, because of God's mercy and human repentance, does not take place.[59] The two elements of apocalypse, *parousia,* "presence" or "coming," and *apocalypsis,* "revelation," have to do with the presence, the coming, the revelation of the other world in this world, but there is also an essential element of uncertainty because "the mercy of God is boundless."

There is already an uncertainty, an equilibrium that comes of uncertainty, in balancing the two worlds off against one anther in a tragic sense of life. "Precisely because it is an interim reading of life," Una Ellis-Fermor says of tragedy, "it speaks to the condition of all but a few at some period of their lives; for it reveals that balance, that uncertainty, which sees two worlds of being and cannot wholly accept either."[60] I think of the experience of living in my imagination because of being unable to accept fully this world of reality in which I find myself, a world of loneliness and aging, but then again being unable to accept fully the other world of eternal life which seems sometimes only a guise of death, as Nietzsche said, taking away the possibility of life and love in this world. To let this world really be and to be open nevertheless to the mystery of the other world seems to change "that balance," to change even "that uncertainty." It moves the center of gravity to the deeper life I can live already in this world. It opens me to an inner light, to a guidance, an enlightenment, an assurance.

I come, like Tolstoy, to understand "The kingdom of God is within you" to mean the other world is here and now in this world, to understand "Christianity not as a mystical doctrine," as he says, a religion merely of the other world, he means, "but as a new life-conception," as a way of life.[61] For me, it is true, this does not mean the other world can be simply reduced to this world, as he seems to think, or that there is no life after death. To say there is one world and it is enough, as I understand it, does not mean the other world does not exist but that it is present already in this world and will be revealed in the consummation of the world — the apocalyptic vision. Still, it does mean, as Tolstoy says, we are to live now as if we were already in the kingdom; it does mean we are not to fight evil with evil, violence with violence; it does mean we are able to live in peace.

"All that we can know is what we who form humanity should or should not do in order to bring about the kingdom of God," Tolstoy says. "And that we all know; for each one has but to begin to do his duty, each one has but to live according to the light that is within him, to bring about the immediate advent of the promised kingdom of God, for which the heart of every man yearns."[62] There is an assurance here, and yet an uncertainty. We know what we should be doing, but we don't know what we will be doing. There is much light in the assurance, much darkness in the uncertainty. If we try to bring about the kingdom of God, as if to make a story come true, we may bring about something we never expected. Vladimir Solovyov answered Tolstoy with "A Short Story of Antichrist," where he has it that Antichrist rather than Christ is the one who brings peace to the world. What Solovyov is saying, it seems, is that there is peace and peace, and that the kind of peace we may bring about may not be the kind of peace we intend or want. Yet in bringing it about we may be nonetheless fulfilling a dark prophecy.

It is the peace of this world that Antichrist brings, according to Solovyov's story, not the peace of the other world in this world. "Peoples of the earth! My peace I give unto you," Antichrist declares. "Henceforth no country will dare to say 'war' when I say 'peace.'"[63] The words are undoubtedly meant to compare and contrast with those in the Gospel of John. "Peace I leave with you; my peace I give to you," Christ says; "not as the world gives do I give to you."[64] The difference here is between words that become facts and words that become flesh. The words of Antichrist are meant to become facts; those of Christ are meant to

become flesh. The peace of Antichrist is a universal peace established by a universal state, like the Pax Romana established by
the Roman Empire. The peace of Christ is a peace in the hearts
of human beings, a peace that turns hearts of stone into hearts
of flesh.

Still, if force is numbing to the heart, if "those who use it
and those who endure it are turned to stone," then it is true, as
Tolstoy was arguing, the peace of Christ is incompatible with
the use of force. There is a "psychic numbing," as Robert Jay
Lifton calls it, that takes place in those who use force and in those
who endure it, a turning of hearts of flesh into hearts of stone.
"Significantly, the capacity for cognition may be retained even
under conditions of advanced numbing," he says; "what is lost
is the symbolic integration which links cognition to feeling and
action."[65] I think of witnessing scenes of violence on film and
television and remaining unmoved. It is as if the numbing takes
place not only in participants, in those who use force and those
who endure it, but also in mere observers, in those who watch
it. The "symbolic integration" of a life is the link that is made
between this world and the other world, all the way from a tragic
sense of life, where feeling for life and death is shaped by the
balance, the uncertainty of the two worlds, to an apocalyptic faith,
where it is shaped by a sense of the presence, the revelation of
the other world in this world.

Just as losing all symbolic integration of the two worlds re-
duces the world to matters of fact and turns the heart to stone,
so gaining or regaining symbolic integration, oftentimes by telling the story of the loss, turns the heart again to flesh. I think
of survivors' tales, "And I only am escaped alone to tell thee,"
as is said in the Book of Job and at the end of *Moby Dick.*[66] For
there is something in the very loss itself, in the undergoing, in
the surviving that moves toward reintegration. Survival, Gabriel
Marcel says, is "an underliving . . . [in] which we advance always
more bent, more torn away from ourselves toward the moment
in which all will be engulfed in love."[67] There is a dynamism in
survival, he is saying, that moves toward what we have been calling "presence" and "revelation." It goes at least as far as the un-

requited longing in a tragic sense of life. It has still then to go the distance from longing to love.

Metaphors of such a change, from stone to flesh, from the flesh of longing to the flesh of love, have been called "mutative metaphors"[68] in psychotherapy, for they not only give expression to the change but help to bring it about. Say I have been living the life of a survivor, like a widow or a widower, a life of grief, going through the loneliness of one who has survived the loss of others or the lack of others in one's life. "And I only am escaped alone to tell thee"—there is loneliness in that sentence, "only" and "alone," and if I "tell thee" I am telling a story of loneliness. Something happens to me, though, as I tell the story. It is like hearing the story of others and their struggle against melancholy, more helpful in my sorrow than a simple story of joy. Telling my story, nevertheless, is like giving thanks. "If one had nothing more to do with God than to be thankful," Meister Eckhart says, "that would be enough."[69] I recollect my own past in the tranquillity of the story, and in that tranquillity emotion itself is transformed, and I pass, as in the Psalms, from mourning to dancing.

Say I could not speak of my feelings till now but could only speak of facts. If I tell the story that envelops these facts, I am saying "the two worlds are really one," for the story brings the dead to life, brings the living and the dead together in one world. I am also saying "figure and ground can be reversed," for I am no longer the lonely figure I was, a surface shape visually appreciable and separable from my surroundings, but as the story goes on I become more and more grounded and inseparable from my grounding. I am saying "the whole is more than a sum of the parts,"[70] the story is more than a sum of matters of fact, the truth of my life is more than the simple facts of my life, for God, as the Kikuyu say in Africa, is not only "the divider" but also "the one who shines."[71] The truth not only divides world from world, figure from ground, whole into parts, but shines in the story as one.

God is "the divider," the one I meet when I confront the truth of my life, when I feel the separation, the loneliness, the fragmentation. Or "the word of God" is the divider, "is living and active, sharper than any two-edged sword, piercing to the division of soul and spirit, of joints and marrow, and discerning the thoughts and intentions of the heart."[72] For when I feel the division of this world from the other, when I know "there are two," it is then "I say there is only one and it is enough." When I feel the loneliness of being a figure separable from its surroundings, it is then I am on the way to being "transparently grounded" in God. When I feel the fragmentation of my life, it is then I am ready to learn to love, to understand what it is to love with every fragment of your being, "with all your heart, and with all your soul, and with all your might." It is rather when I cannot feel the division, the isolation, the brokenness, when I can feel only the not-feeling, the numbness, that I have no sense of meeting God, no awareness of presence or of revelation, but only of numbing violence, of force.

God is "the one who shines" then when I say Yes to God "the divider," when I let myself feel the division, the loneliness, the brokenness. Then the world becomes one, I am grounded in God, and I become able to love. And I let myself feel when I give expression to feeling, when I tell the story, even a story of force, of violence. Calling the *Iliad* "the poem of force," Simone Weil speaks of its "bitterness that proceeds from tenderness and that spreads over the whole human race, impartial as sunlight."[73] If I can feel and yet be impartial, if I can go from passion to compassion in telling the story, from passion where there is a kindling of the heart to compassion where the kindling becomes an illumining, even though the illumining takes place only after the fact, only in the story, then I begin to know "the one who shines."

Apocalyptic faith itself changes from passion to compassion, from a passionate to a compassionate hope, when I realize we are in a story, when I reflect on the unknowing there is in being in a story that is still taking place, on the uncertainty of living among prophetic warnings when the mercy of God is boundless. I can lose passion in going over to compassion. "To be aware that one is burning is to grow cold; to feel an intensity is to diminish it," Bachelard says; "it is necessary to be an intensity without real-

izing it."[74] When I pass over from passion to compassion, I lose
some of the "blessed assurance"[75] of apocalyptic faith, I become
like Jonah, aware that all promises and all warnings are overshadowed by the boundless mercy of God. Still, the illumining
that takes place in compassion is an illumining of the heart not
just of the mind. I am indeed aware that I am burning, I do
indeed feel the intensity, but that means the fire is becoming light.
The God who is a consuming fire is becoming life and light and
love for me. There is still a "blessed assurance," but it is the
assurance of mercy.

It is like the tempering of love by compassion. When love
is untempered, it can be consuming. "To be loved means to be
consumed," Rilke says. "To love is to give light with inexhaustible oil. To be loved is to pass away, to love is to endure."[76] When
I love with untempered love, I feel my own feelings but I do not
feel the feelings of the other person. I am consuming the other
person in my love while I myself am burning with inexhaustible
oil. When I pass over to the standpoint of the other person, though,
I begin to feel the other's feelings. I become aware that I am burning, I begin to feel the intensity myself, and the fire begins to
change into light. I learn "to penetrate the beloved object with
the rays of feeling," as Rilke says, "rather than consuming it in
them."[77] I become able to see beyond my love, to see beyond my
anger at the other's failure to return my love.

So it is with the tempering of hope. When I seek a "blessed
assurance," when I seek certainty, I become ever more uncer-
tain, and I have to keep denying all the doubts that come to my
mind. When I pass over from a quest of certainty to a quest of
understanding, though, I open myself to a more universal hope,
a hope for everyone and not just for me and mine. I come to
a light that I would have taken for darkness:

> I said to the man who stood at the gate of the year, "Give
> me a light that I may tread safely into the unknown." And he
> replied, "Go out into the darkness and put your hand into the
> hand of God. That shall be to you better than light and safer
> than a known way."[78]

At first I seek the light of certainty, "a light that I may tread safely into the unknown." But then I find the way of understanding, of being led by God in the darkness of uncertainty, a way that is "better than light and safer than a known way." It is not that I truly possessed "blessed assurance" and then lost it. I have not lost certainty so much as the quest of certainty. I have been learning instead to see in the dark. Here is the answer to my question, "What do I know of the unknown?"

Faith is seeing light with your heart, it is said, *when all your eyes see is darkness.* That becomes more and more consciously true, it seems, as you pass over from passion to compassion. Thus when Gandhi says "There have been tyrants and murderers, and for a time they can seem invincible. But in the end they always fall" and "When I despair, I remember that all through history the way of truth and love has always won," he is not simply stating a fact. He is giving expression rather to his faith. He is seeing light with his heart when all his eyes see is darkness. An apocalyptic faith is no different; it is a seeing of light with the heart, the light of presence, of coming, of revelation, when all the eyes see is darkness, war and famine and plague and death. It is not the darkness that the eyes see that is the matter of faith, the threat of nuclear war for instance, but the light that the heart sees, the peace of God.

3

Waiting on Love

———

The single requirement the spiritual father lays down for the acceptance of a postulant is that he should have sensed in his heart, even though it be only once, a feeling of love for God.
　　　　　　　　　　　　　　　　　　　　—Matta el-Meskeen

Yet what if God were impersonal? What if the highest relation with God were not an "I and thou" but simply a oneness with God? Gandhi's saying can seem to point in that direction, "God never occurs to you in person but always in action."[1] Still, Gandhi's way was one of waiting on God, of waiting for God to lead and then following in God's way, of listening to "the inner voice," as he called it, and letting it direct his life.

Waiting on God is like waiting on love. "I adjure you, O daughters of Jerusalem," it is said three times in the Song of Solomon, "that you stir not up nor awaken love until it please."[2] Waiting on love, letting it come when it comes, letting it go when it goes, is the opposite of using or trying to use love, of betraying love, of throwing love away. What could ever bring one to sacrifice a great love? Pride, the fear of becoming a fool of love. That is the conclusion Leo Perutz comes to in his novel *Leonardo's Judas*. Leonardo da Vinci is looking for a model of Judas for his painting of the Last Supper, someone capable like Judas of betraying the one he loves. It cannot be someone who is incapable of love. It has to be someone who loves but throws love away. It cannot be the miser Boccetta, for example. "How could he be a Judas, for there's not a soul in the world whom he loves," a boy tells Leonardo, a boy whose father Boccetta drove to suicide. "You know Judas' secret?" Leonardo asks. "You know why he betrayed Christ?" "He betrayed Him when he realized he loved Him," the boy replies. "He could see that he was going to love Him too much, and his pride would not permit that."[3]

As you go with Leonardo in this story, looking for one who loves and is loved but who throws love away, you have the uneasy feeling that you are the one he is looking for. The one he finds is the merchant Behaim, who betrays the beautiful Niccola's love rather than be cheated out of a debt by Boccetta, her miserly father. You wonder if you have not somehow done the same thing, if the words addressed to Behaim could not also be addressed to you, "So you threw away a great love like a cheap ring bought at a flea market."[4] What is "a great love"? One in which you are able to be heart and soul in love. Are you willing to be heart and soul in a love of man and woman? That was the question for Behaim. Are you willing to be heart and soul in the love of Christ? That was the question for Judas. Are you willing to be heart and soul in the love of God? That was the question for Leonardo himself in all he did, the question of every great love.

To be or not to be a fool of love, that is the question for pride here. Waiting on inspiration, waiting on love, waiting on God, I may well ask myself, as Leonardo often does in his notebooks, thinking of his unfinished works, "Tell me if anything has ever been accomplished."[5] That is always the question on an unviolent way. Let us see what difference it makes in action to wait on the kindling and illumining of the heart. Let us see what there is when there is as yet no kindling, no illumining.

"If there is no love, what then?"

"If there is no love, what then?"[6] Leonardo asked himself in a time of distress when he seemed to be without any friends. Waiting on love is waiting on connection with others, on connection with the universe, on the empowerment that comes of connection. Say I have no deep feeling for anyone or anything. Say there is nothing important I share, dwelling with, traveling with others. Say there is no profound tie or relationship I have with anyone or anything. "If there is no love, what then?" Then I am isolated and powerless. Waiting on love then means waiting on that feeling I don't have, that sharing, that tie or relationship; expecting it with some certainty, making preparations for it, anticipating its particulars in my mind, or again hoping for it without certainty but with confidence, even assurance that it will come; looking to it, free of doubt, or looking for it with less assurance but with an expectancy, a watchfulness; or simply awaiting it, being ready for it, and it awaiting me.

Is there a great love in my life? If there is, then I am awaiting it but it also is awaiting me. When I say "it is awaiting me," I mean love is there before you realize it. There is certainly a great loneliness in my life, and if loneliness is love or if loneliness becomes love, then there is a great love. It is at the transition point from loneliness to love that the danger of betraying love arises. "He betrayed Him when he realized he loved Him," the boy told Leonardo. "He could see that he was going to love Him too much, and his pride would not permit that." At the transition point you realize you love, and then you have to choose whether to give or to withhold your heart. If you withhold your heart, there is a movement from the betrayal of love to despair, as in the story of Judas. If you give your heart, there is a movement from faithfulness to faith.

"I am without any of my friends,"[7] Leonardo had written in his time of distress, and that is perhaps what prompted him to ask "If there is no love, what then?" There is loneliness, I say, but it is this very loneliness you feel, when you are without any of your friends, that becomes love. It is the longing in the loneliness that becomes the love, I mean, the longing to be unalone, the longing for union or reunion. If I am faithful myself, even when I feel betrayed or abandoned, I can make the transition from loneliness to love, and as I remain faithful, staying with my loneliness, living in my loneliness without despairing, I pass from faithfulness to faith, for that is what faith is, living in uncertainty without despairing. It is when I am not faithful myself, when I do not stay in my loneliness with hope, that I lose all faith in love, no longer believing in the friendship of my friends, no longer relying on the love of God. If I stay with my loneliness without despairing, I come to believe that I am not alone. I come to believe in love, for I can feel the love in myself.

Is this really love, though, this longing, or is it only loneliness? If there is a great loneliness in my life, does that mean there is a great love? Violence too is an answer to the question, "If there is no love, what then?" It is an answer that arises out of the despair of love. Let me see if I can get past the doubt and the despair, if I can find the way from loneliness to love. I have an idea that the contemplative life is the secret of passage, that violence and numbing of heart arise in the absence, and love and kindling of heart arise in the presence of contemplation.

"We are to do nothing but wait," Heidegger says, speaking of contemplation, though his thought has been described as "without love."[8] It is a thinking that falls short of love but is on the way. "We are to do nothing but wait" — he says it in a conversation with a scholar and a scientist. "That is poor consolation," the scholar replies. "Poor or not," he answers, "we should not await consolation — something we would still be doing if we became disconsolate." We should be *waiting,* he is saying, as if we knew nothing, not *awaiting* as if we knew what we were waiting for. Yet what if consolation is awaiting us, what if we are awaiting love and love is awaiting us? When we wait as if we knew nothing, we are waiting to know. When we wait as if it were awaiting us, we are reaching beyond knowledge, we are waiting to love. "We must find silence so then we can find ideas of ourselves and others," a friend once wrote to me, "not ideas of words but of silent eggs that enter our thoughts and open and grow." There is a knowing that comes of loving, and that is the knowing that is sought in contemplation, a knowing that reaches into the silence out of which words arise. In the silence we come to love.

"When every word is an enigma,"[9] as in Heidegger's thinking, and the method is to trace every word back to the silence out of which it arises, thinking is on the way to love, even if it is not directed toward love. There is a step however to be taken, and that is to let silence speak. How is that to be done when one is using words? There is a way, for there is always something untold in telling, there is always a silence that can speak in the telling of a story. "Where the story-teller is loyal, eternally and unswervingly loyal to the story, there, in the end, silence will speak," Isak Dinesen says. "Where the story has been betrayed, silence is but emptiness."[10] If there is a mystery, an enigma, in a story and I tell the story, allowing the mystery to show itself and at the same time to withdraw, as mystery always does, then I am being faithful to the story and the silence will speak.

Say I am telling the Christian story, like Leonardo painting the Last Supper, telling it in words, telling it in deeds. If I let the mystery show itself and at the same time hide itself, I am being loyal to the story, and the silence will speak to me, and in the silence I may hope to find love. I have to wait on the mystery, though, like Leonardo spending hours just looking at the unfinished painting. If I become impatient with the mystery, taking its showing and withdrawing to be an intolerable game of hide-and-seek, I may betray the story in my words, betray the mystery in my deeds, like Leonardo's Judas. The words of Christ to Martha are a key, "you are anxious and troubled about many things; one thing is needful."[11] It is true, I am anxious and troubled about many things. If I do recognize the one thing, nevertheless, the mystery, as Martha did, I am being faithful to the story, even though my anxiety about the many things means I have still to complete the movement from faithfulness to faith. If I complete the movement, if I let go of the many and devote myself to the one, like her sister Mary "who sat at the Lord's feet and listened to his teaching,"[12] my waiting becomes love.

"In waiting we leave open what we are waiting for,"[13] Heidegger says. Waiting, as he conceives it, is thinking, but nonrepresentational thinking, and thus a thinking that leaves open what it is waiting for, a thinking of Being rather than of beings, of the one rather than of the many. If I let go of the many and devote myself to the one, I am leaving open what I am waiting for insofar as I am letting the one, the mystery, show itself as it will and hide itself as it will. I am following the adjuration "that you stir not up nor awaken love until it please." There is no will in waiting, according to Heidegger, and thus for him waiting remains thinking and never becomes loving. There is will, I want to say, or rather willingness that allows love to awaken, that allows the heart to be kindled, and so contemplation becomes a thinking that is a loving, a loving that is a thinking.

Will in waiting is willingness, the willingness to give myself heart and soul, like Mary's willingness to sit at the Lord's feet and listen to his teaching. There is affect even in waiting without will, "exulting in waiting," as Heidegger says; there is even willingness, "steadfastness" that "could be said perhaps to correspond to the highest willing."[14] So in fact simple openness to the mystery verges upon devotion to the mystery, even though one does not want to speak of will. If I recognize the role of willingness, however, I come to realize I am making a choice in devoting myself. And something does truly happen when the choice becomes conscious. It is like realizing I am in love. I was in love already when I was simply waiting on love, when I was conscious only of being lonely, but now that I realize it, now that I choose it, I go from being in love to loving. I say Yes to love of the mystery itself. That is the love that transforms loneliness, that seizes your whole being, all your heart and soul and might, that calls you from the many, that calls you to the one.

I visited a monastery once in the desert in Egypt, a Coptic monastery where the only requirement for one who wishes to enter and become a monk is to have felt the love of God: "the single requirement is that he should have sensed in his heart, even though it be only once, a feeling of love for God."[15] I wondered when I heard this if some persons, only some, feel the love of God and others do not. As I thought about it, I came to believe that everyone has that feeling at some time, "even though it be only once," but not everyone recognizes the feeling for what it is. It is one thing to have such a feeling, and it is another to recognize it as a feeling of love, and it is still another to name it a feeling of love for God. There is choice here. There is a choosing in allowing oneself to have the feeling at all. There is a choosing also in recognizing it. And there is a choosing in naming it.

One's choice may be to reject love, like Leonardo's Judas, "and his love died, murdered by his will, betrayed by his pride."[16] What one loses in rejecting love, Perutz suggests, is the chance to "rejoin the whole." There is a figure in his story, Mancino the old poet, who seems to be none other than the great François

Villon, lost and bereft of his memory. He is in love with Niccola but is too old for her, and is in his own eyes an old fool of love, as in the proverb "No fool like an old fool." He remains true, nevertheless, to his unrequited love, and when he dies trying to do a service for her, Leonardo says "Die? I think of it differently. He has proudly rejoined the whole and thus escaped from earthly imperfection."[17] Thus love, true love, is ultimately love of God, I gather, for to love, and to die, is to let go of one's separate existence and to rejoin the whole of existence. There is pride in refusing love, that of one's separate existence, but there is pride also in choosing to love, that of one who has "proudly rejoined the whole," a pride that is humility, a willingness to join the human race.

It is true, one who has "proudly rejoined the whole" has joined more than the human race. The feeling one has when one has "sensed in his heart, even though it be only once, a feeling of love for God" is a feeling for the whole. Thus it is that you are able to love "with all your heart, and with all your soul, and with all your might." The whole of existence evokes the whole human being. I think of the setting sun as I walk along the seashore, how its light, while shining on all, seems to form a trail over the water leading directly to me, following me as I walk. If I allow myself to have a feeling for the whole, if I come to recognize something greater than myself to which I belong, if I name it God, I enter into a personal relationship with it, as if its light flowed directly to me, following me, leading me in the course of my life.

No doubt, the light of the sun creates a path to me over the water only in my perception. It creates a similar path to everyone else walking along the shore, and follows each of us as we walk by one another, as if the paths of light were crisscrossing as we pass each other. So it is too with the light of God or of the whole. It flows to me in my perception of it, in the kindling of my heart and the illumining of my mind. Yet that is real enough and true enough for me to enter into a personal relationship with God, a to-and-fro with the whole. It is because of the personal relationship, the to-and-fro, that I use the personal name

"God" as well as the impersonal name "the whole." But is the whole the same as God? Yes, if the whole is more than a sum of the parts. "He has proudly rejoined the whole," the sentence reads, "and thus escaped from earthly imperfection." If the whole is free of earthly imperfection, then it is "all" in all-knowing, all-powerful, all-merciful. It is all in all. I think of Walt Whitman's words, "and to die is different from what any one supposed and luckier."[18]

Proud and lucky! To love and to die, to let go of my separate existence, is "different from what any one supposed" who had not yet let go, "and luckier," for it is not the destruction but the fulfillment of myself, as Whitman sings in *Song of Myself.* The letting go is really an entering into relationship. It is letting go of isolation, of unrelatedness. The choice in love and death is between letting go and holding on, between willingness and unwillingness. It is not a choice of love, a choice of death, as if love and death were in my power, but a choice of relationship, of how I shall relate to love and to death. If the whole is the mystery, the unknown that shows and hides itself in love and in death, the choice I am making is how to take the unknown in life, how to take the prospect of rejoining the whole. Proud and lucky?

If to rejoin the whole is not to lose my identity but to enter into a relation with the whole, if it is to lose only separateness and to gain relatedness, then indeed it is proud and lucky. This supposes my identity is in my relatedness rather than my separateness, in who I am rather than who I am not. It was said of Leonardo during life he was "such that his work was hindered by his desire," by "the wish ever to seek excellence upon excellence, and perfection upon perfection."[19] His relationship with the whole during life was one of desire, that is, and this hindered him, causing him to leave one thing unfinished while he turned to another. But I think the unfinished works show also the quality of his waiting, as Perutz suggests, waiting to find the face of Judas, for instance, gazing for hours at the unfinished painting of the Last Supper, waiting on inspiration. To achieve all in a human lifetime would be impossible; to receive all as a gift, though, as the consummation of life in eternal life would be to rejoin the whole. To attain to the whole during life would be to discover it step by step, inspiration by inspiration, on a journey always unfinished.

"For painting is the way to learn to know the maker of all marvelous things — and this is the way to love so great an inventor," Leonardo says. "For in truth great love springs from the full knowledge of the thing that one loves; and if you do not know it you can love it but little or not at all."[20] To know is to love, he is saying, to know God is to love God, and to paint and to invent is to perceive the unimaginable hand and mind of God at their work. Unfinished work, like Leonardo's own painting and inventing, hindered as it is by desire, is nonetheless successful in his coming to know God and to love God. By doing, by making, you come to know God in the act of creating, to see things as God sees them, to see their beauty, and thus by seeing what God sees and doing what God does, by loving what you see and do, you come to love God. Here is "great love," and it comes of "full knowledge."

To let go of separate existence, to rejoin the whole, "to love, I wonder whether it is possible to him," Paul Valery says of Leonardo. I wonder whether it is possible to me, whether I am willing and able to let go of myself so far as to rejoin the whole. "Nevertheless he must find in himself some landmarks so placed as to bring his private life and this generalized life which he has discovered in himself into harmony with each other."[21] This "harmony" is like the trail of light I see coming to me from the sun over the water. There is the universal life I discover, the sunlight I see shining on all; there is the personal life I live, walking up and down the seashore; and there is the connection between the two, the trail of light over the water, following me as I walk. To know, according to this, is to be aware not only of my own life but of the universal life encompassing my own. This is Leonardo's "full knowledge." To love then is to let go of the isolation of my personal life, to let my life be encompassed by the greater life, to bring my life and the universal life into harmony. This is his "great love."

Those "landmarks" Valery speaks of, "so placed as to bring

his private life and this generalized life he has discovered in himself into harmony," for me are moments of inspiration, of kindling of heart, of illumining of mind, when the universal life flows in upon my personal life. These moments mark the boundary between my own life and the encompassing life of all; they serve to guide me in steering my course in life; they mark the course I have taken and can be used as points of orientation in charting the course I shall take. They are moments of exaltation. What if I were to live in that exaltation? "His joy is to be nothing, to do nothing, to think nothing," Yeats says of the saint, "but to permit the total life, expressed in its humanity, to flow in upon him and to express itself through his acts and thoughts."[22] What he is describing, it seems, is really one who has "proudly rejoined the whole."

So there are moments when I do rejoin the whole, when my joy is to let the total life flow in upon me and express itself in my acts and thoughts. There are times in between those moments, though, when Leonardo's question is mine, "If there is no love, what then?" I wonder, at those times between, if I am willing and able to let go of my own autonomy so far as to love. In moments of inspiration, on the other hand, I am caught up in a life that is greater than myself and letting go seems only a matter of consenting to what is already happening. Autonomy is the crucial thing here, the ability to do things for yourself that you begin to acquire in childhood and begin to lose in old age, but more than that, the ability to think for yourself and to decide for yourself. There is the autonomy of reason, the autonomy of conscience, and yet in the illumining of the mind the autonomous reason becomes "the inner light," and in the kindling of the heart the autonomous conscience becomes "the inner voice." "But the time has come," I feel like saying then, "I am being swept off my feet at last."[23]

I feel a longing to love and be loved, sometimes so strongly that it clarifies my feelings about others, to the point of realizing it is relatedness I desire, not just encounter or temporary contact. In such moments of clarity, I realize it is not just moments I am seeking but something that is abiding. I realize at the same time my life is passing, all things are passing. If I keep on going from encounter to passing encounter, from contact to temporary contact, I will come in the end to nothing. Unless the restless movement itself is love. If I name it love, the love of God, I become aware of a growing light, "By waiting and by calm you shall be saved; in quiet and in trust your strength lies."[24] By waiting and by calm, in quiet and in trust, I find abiding love, by resting, that is, in the restless movement of the heart.

"Love is a direction"

"It is only necessary to know that love is a direction and not a state of soul," Simone Weil says. "If one is unaware of this, one falls into despair at the first onslaught of affliction."[25] There is a direction in waiting and in trust, and if one is aware of it and knows it is the direction of love, one is able to dwell in it calmly and quietly, resting even in movement, knowing it is one's strength and one's salvation. If one is unaware of it, aware only of restless movement, one is vulnerable to despair, fearing one's life will come to nothing, a series of passing encounters. A friend once said of romantic love, "If it is intimate, it cannot be lasting, and if it is lasting, it cannot be intimate." That was from reading stories of romance where love is more "a state of soul," a feeling, than "a direction," an orientation of life. Love is a direction, I want to say: sometimes felt and thus also a state of soul, sometimes unfelt and thus only a direction. It is the state of soul, the feeling, that is not lasting; it is the direction, the orientation, that is not intimate when unfelt, yet intimate when felt.

When Leonardo's Judas was thinking of betraying his love, he was afraid he would not be able to get rid of the feeling of love. "I shall have to turn my heart to stone. But can I? Don't I still love her?"[26] Then he decided, "and his love died, murdered by his will, betrayed by his pride." Still he could not get his love out of his mind. "And your love for her, or what you called your love, is it now completely dead?" he was asked. "I have not got her out of my mind yet . . ." he answered, "But I think I shall stop thinking about her. . . ."[27] He changed the direction of his life, and thus "his love died, murdered by his will," but he could not easily forget the feeling of love. So love is a direction, one that can be abandoned by one's will, and yet it is also a state of soul, intimate and sometimes lasting, even against one's will.

It is lasting in memory. Thus it is possible to remember love and possible also to forget it, and then again, after forgetting, to remember it once more. It is lasting and not lasting. That is true even of "a feeling of love for God." It is not lasting if one has sensed it in one's heart "only once," and yet it is lasting "even though it be only once," for it lives in one's memory. It has become emotion to be recollected in tranquillity. Say I have had the conviction that nothing happens without the will of God. I think of the people who live on the altiplano of Peru and Bolivia —when some terrible thing happens, how they say *Dios quiere,* "God wills," or *Dios lo quiere,* "God wills it," but with the overtones of *quiere* in Spanish, "wills" or "loves," as if the love of God were in the will of God, and thus if God's will is there in the unknown in life, however terrible, then God's love is also there. Say I too have this feeling of a will that is loving, and I have on my part the feeling of a love that is willing. Sensing God's love, I feel a love for God. I go from memory to understanding to will.

Is the love in my memory, a will that is loving, the same as the love in my will, a love that is willing? Is the love in my will simply a Yes to the will of God? Or is it the very love of God itself? I think of a poem by Gabriela Mistral entitled *Dios Lo Quiere,* [28] a love poem of desolation where she cries out against the spurning of her love by the one she loves, where she is saying "God wills our love" or "God loves our love." Somehow human love and the love of God are one. If there is a great love in my life, I will find it in the memory of love, in the will to love, and in the understanding that links will to memory.

Speaking of desolation, Simone Weil says if we remain in our desolation "without ceasing to love, we end by touching something that is not affliction, not joy, something that is the central essence, necessary and pure, something not of the senses, common to joy and sorrow: the very love of God."[29] If it is true that God wills our love, that God loves our love, then if we continue to love, even in the midst of desolation when we feel only our loneliness, if we are faithful, we come to faith. And we end by touching God's will in us, feeling God's love in us, as if our desolation, our loneliness, were a nakedness, like the nakedness of Adam and Eve after the fall, that exposes us and leaves us vulnerable to God, that allows us to touch God or allows God to touch us, if we do not hide ourselves from God, as Adam and Eve did in their shame. Desolation and loneliness, to be sure, is the feeling of God's absence, the feeling at any rate of joy's absence. But "we end by touching something that is not affliction, not joy," something "common to joy and sorrow." We end by touching the presence in the absence, God in no God.

If it is common to joy and sorrow, though, the love of God can be found also in joy. "We know then that joy is the sweetness of contact with the love of God," Weil goes on to say, "that affliction is the wound of this same contact when it is painful, and that only the contact matters, not the manner of it."[30] That must be the true meaning of *Dios lo quiere,* contact with the love of God, whether it is sweet or painful. As I search through time and memory, therefore, I search for God both in joy and in sorrow. I readily find joy and sorrow, but do I find the love of God? Joy and sorrow stand out by their contrast. The love of God, if it is common to joy and sorrow, is not so easy to discern. It is like the light of our eyes. Yet I have a sense of its being very powerful, capable of causing great joy and great sorrow.

It can be like violence, when you are unwilling, only it kindles instead of numbing the heart. I think of Flannery O'Connor's novel, *The Violent Bear It Away,* named after the saying of Jesus, "From the days of John the Baptist until now, the kingdom of heaven suffereth violence, and the violent bear it away."[31] The story revolves around an idiot child whose very existence seems to challenge the concept of a rational universe. The only thing commensurate with the child seems to be the madness of the old man, his uncle, who thinks himself a prophet and the similar madness of the boy, his cousin, who succeeds the uncle as prophet and ends up baptising the child while drowning him in the lake. Even the child's father, otherwise committed to a rational universe, is tempted by the madness, feeling at times "a love for the child so outrageous that he would be left shocked and depressed for days, and trembling for his sanity." It is the mystery of the child that evokes this madness, this love. "It was love without reason, love for something futureless, love that appeared to exist only to be itself, imperious and all demanding, the kind that would cause him to make a fool of himself in an instant."[32] The mystery of the child opened out upon the mystery of all, and the love "only began with" the child, "and then like an avalanche covered everything his reason hated."

It is love of the mystery, the unknown in life. It is like falling in love, where one is drawn to "an unknown life" (*une vie inconnue*),[33] as Marcel Proust says, that one perceives in the other person, and one wants to be with the other to share in that life. Only here the mystery of the other person opens out upon the mystery of all, and one falls in love, as it were, with the mystery of all, one falls in love with God. It is a love that calls one to change the whole direction of one's will and one's life. I think of Karl Rahner's words about mystery,

> . . . it is at once a menace to man and his blessed peace. It can make him chafe and protest, because it compels him to leave the tiny house of his ostensibly clear self-possession, to advance into the trackless spaces, even in the night. It seems to ask too much of him, to overburden him with monstrous claims. It forces upon him the dilemma of either throwing himself into the uncharted, unending adventure where he commits himself to the infinite, or — despairing at the thought and so embittered — of taking shelter in the suffocating den of his own finite perspicacity.[34]

That is what the mystery is in *The Violent Bear It Away*, a "menace" and a "blessed peace," and in the end it bears the violent away, taming their wild hearts, or better, kindling their numbed hearts. Thus when the boy at the end consents to his call to be a prophet, he hears the words in his heart, "Go warn the children of God of the terrible speed of mercy."[35] Here is the mystery, "the terrible speed of mercy," the mystery in war and famine and plague and death as well as in peace and nourishment and healing and life. It is the unknown in life, the element of the unknown, but taken in the light of a faith in the boundless mercy of God. If faithfulness is the way to faith, there is a transition here from the slowness that is experienced in faithfulness, in waiting, to the speed that is experienced in faith, in the coming of love. It is as though there were long time spans involved in loneliness, while there is a kind of suddenness in love, as though I had spent a long time being lonely and being faithful in my loneliness, while all this is changed in a moment when someone comes into my life.

Or it is changed simply by the kindling of my heart and the illumining of my mind, by "joy without a cause" or "consolation without any preceding cause."[36] But here I am tending again to identify the love of God with joy and with consolation and to forget what Simone Weil said, "joy is the sweetness of contact with the love of God," and "affliction is the wound of this same contact when it is painful" and "only the contact matters, not the manner of it." If both joy and affliction come as mercy, as contact with the love of God, then indeed the speed of mercy is "terrible" and those words "the terrible speed of mercy" are on a par with *Dios lo quiere.* It makes sense then to say "Go warn the children of God of the terrible speed of mercy." For it is not only a promise but also a warning.

Why do things have to be this way? Why is contact with the love of God sometimes sweet and sometimes painful? I think it is because of the orientation of the will. When there is a conflict of the human will with the will of God, there is suffering. That is true even of the agony of Christ in the garden when he prays, "not as I will, but as thou wilt,"[37] for even though he is submitting his will to that of God he still feels the conflict. Here is where the understanding arises that links will to memory, out of this "why," out of this conflict of wills. It is an openness of the mind to mystery. "But the mystery is the sole peace of him who trusts himself to it, loves it humbly, and surrenders himself to it fearlessly in knowledge and love," Rahner says. "The mystery is eternal light and eternal peace."[38] Or it becomes light and peace to a mind that is opened to it. If I trust myself to the mystery, to the unknown in life, if I love it humbly and surrender myself to it fearlessly in knowledge and love, I enter into a relationship with God, an "I and thou" as in "not as I will, but as thou wilt," a union of wills.

Understanding comes of releasing the grip of will on understanding. I think of another story by Leo Perutz, according to which there is a moment when God comes, *Dios viene,* when what we bring about is not what we had in mind. A town in Spain has been occupied by two regiments of Napoleon's army. The Marquis of Bolibar goes into the town in disguise to rouse it against Napoleon's soldiers and yield it to Spanish guerrillas. He overhears the secret of a group of officers, how they have all been lovers of the colonel's wife, and is taken by them to be shot, but he begs them for God's sake to let him find someone to complete his task. Not knowing what it is, they say they will do it. "You will do it for me?" he cries. "You?" Then the church bell rings, and he says in a low, reverent voice, *Dios viene,* "God is coming."[39] And so he goes to his death, and they, unwittingly, go on to bring about their own destruction.

Love is a direction but one that remains unknown until we let go of the intentions we have superimposed. It is a direction that can destroy us, as in the story, if we cling to our own purposes and let it work only at unawares. To rejoin the whole is where love takes us, but that is only death and destruction when it takes us there against our own will. The Marquis of Bolibar let go of his cause, let God take up his cause, in that moment when he said *Dios viene,* "God is coming." Then he rose up, all doubt and fear put aside, and went proudly to his death, "proudly rejoined the whole." With that the narrator of the story began to feel doubt and fear, "God had come. . . . A shiver ran through me, together with a dread of something that could not be put into words — something that loomed before me as dark, menacing and fraught with danger as the gloomy shadows of those distant oak forests."[40] I think of the moment in Isak Dinesen's story of her life in Africa when her servant awakened her after midnight with the words "Msabu, I think that you had better get up. I think that God is coming."[41]

It was a grass-fire coming, as she explained to him. "Well yes," he said, "it may be so. But I thought that you had better get up in case it was God coming." It is not simply a matter of fact that God is coming. It is a fact rather that a grass-fire is coming. To say "God is coming" is to speak of our relationship with the matter of fact. Thus the servant says "I think that you had better get up." I have to awaken, to get up, in order to enter into a relationship with the matter of fact. It is a kind of dullness, according to this, simply to note matters of fact and not enter into relationship with them. If I do enter into a relationship, then it can well seem that I am dealing with Someone rather than simply with Something. There is a saying, though, among the Kikuyu, the people among whom Dinesen was living, "God is not to be pestered," *Ngai ndagiagiagwo,*[42] as if to say the relationship is not to be too personal.

How personal or impersonal a relationship is to be is a matter of hope and of willingness. If there is willingness but little or no hope, then the relationship is more impersonal. Speaking of this Kikuyu saying, Jomo Kenyatta says

> It has wide implications. In the first place it implies that even if a terrible calamity, such as the death of his child, should befall a man, his attitude must be one of resignation, for the people know that Ngai gives and has the power to take away. The man is not left hopeless, for Ngai may restore his losses—another child may be born to him.[43]

The attitude is to be one of willingness, he is saying, of "resignation," and yet one is "not left hopeless." If there is a strong hope, however, combined with willingness, then the relationship is much more personal, and God may even be pestered, as in the parable of the unjust judge who says "Though I neither fear God nor regard man, yet because this widow bothers me, I will vindicate her, or she will wear me out by her continual coming," or in the parable of the friend bothered at night, of whom Jesus says "I tell you, though he will not get up and give him anything be- cause he is his friend, yet because of his importunity he will rise and give him whatever he needs."[44] In fact, in this pestering of God the element of willingness can almost disappear in the face of such persistent hope. Thus when the Marquis of Bolibar prayed, "He bellowed at the Almighty, sometimes angrily, sometimes threateningly, and sometimes as if striving to bully Him into doing his, Bolibar's, will."[45]

Human relations with God can range thus from willing- ness with only slight hope to hope with only slight willingness. Yet there is always some hope and some willingness, some hope even after saying "God is not to be pestered," some sense that one is "not left hopeless," and some willingness even after crying out "Do you hear me, Lord?" like the Marquis of Bolibar, some submission as when he went down on his knees and said *Dios viene,* "God is coming." If love is a direction that can be felt as a longing in the heart, the willingness to let go of the many hopes and intentions that obscure the direction makes way for the more fundamental hope that the heart's longing will be fulfilled. Thus when the Marquis of Bolibar lets go of his cause and lets God take up his cause, he gives up control but he does not give up his heart's desire.

What if I were to give up hope? What if I were to hold to my own will? Then I would be giving in to the dread and fasci- nation of nothingness, a dread and fascination like that of death. If there is no hope, if there is only my own will, there is a kind of nothingness in place of God. It is true, God is not merely a thing, is no thing, as it were, can be experienced as an empti- ness, a void, as in Buddhism, but a void that is full of grace. For as Simone Weil says, "grace fills empty spaces."[46] If I live in hope and willingness, I am living out of grace rather than out of nothingness. The questions I asked, "What if I were to give up hope? What if I were to hold to my own will?" are like Leo- nardo's question, "If there is no love, what then?" The answer I have found, Simone Weil's answer, "Love is a direction," says there is love if the direction is there, even if it is unfelt. There

is love, I would add, even if it is unhoped and unwilled. So too
God is present, though the presence be unfelt, unhoped, unwilled.
There is a great love in my life, I conclude, *felt or unfelt, hoped or unhoped,
willed or unwilled.*

The thing is to feel it, to hope it, to will it. I realize when
I quote Simone Weil here that she is speaking of a direction that
is willed. I am speaking of a direction that is already there before
you will it, the direction of the heart's longing. Hope and willingness can point in that direction even when you do not feel
it, she is saying. You come to feel it by waiting on it, by waiting
on the kindling of the heart and the illumining of the mind. How
do you come to hope it and to will it? There is hope and willingness in the waiting. After saying "wait without hope," wait
without obscuring the direction of love with the many hopes and
fears that fill your life. T. S. Eliot goes on to say "the faith and
the love and the hope are all in the waiting."[47] The love is there
too, the direction itself, but it is there in the heart's longing, I
would add, even if you are not waiting on love.

There is a being in love, I am saying, that comes before
loving, before consenting, before choosing to love. If I do love,
if I do consent, if I do choose to love, I can become a fool of
love. If consciousness is the direction one is looking and uncon-
sciousness is the direction one is not looking, then the reason
it is hard to look in this direction of love is that one can see oneself becoming a fool of love. I often meditate on that saying, "No
fool like an old fool." I often apply it to myself, thinking of myself like Mancino falling in love with Niccola. It has a deeper
meaning, though, I see now, as I meditate on the love of God.
It is wise to be a fool of love for God. It is foolish to be too wise
to be an old fool. The harshness of the saying falls away, as I
meditate on it, "No fool so wise as an old fool of love for God."
The word "infatuation" means "becoming a fool," and it is true,
there is something foolish about falling in love with someone who
is young when I am old. There is something foolish about falling in love with One who is eternal when I am mortal, and yet
it is a wise folly.

If I become the things I know and love, then I am becoming youthful when I fall in love with youthful beauty and grace, and there is the foolishness, for I am old, and I am becoming eternal when I fall in love with the One who is eternal, and there is the foolishness, for I am mortal. Yet it is a wise foolishness to allow the youth in me to live on, to allow the eternal child to live in me as I am aging. If the foolishness is to be wise, however, I have to learn to love without denying my mortality. I have to learn to love and to die. All the wisdom of this is contained in that saying, "I adjure you, O daughters of Jerusalem, that you stir not up nor awaken love until it please." One rabbinical interpretation is that this is an injunction against forcing the end.[48] If I pass from will to willingness in relation to love and death, if I give up the attempt to force things, the foolishness of my love becomes wise.

To love and to die, to be willing to love and to be willing to die, that is the way to eternal childhood, the way into the kingdom of God. Sometimes the only memory of love one has is from childhood, like Paul Celan's memory of loving the burning candle of the Sabbath, "I loved its burning down, and do you know, I have not loved anything since; no, nothing: or perhaps that which burned down like that candle on that day. . . ."[49] Suddenly the tiny love seems to expand into a great love for all that burned down like that candle on that day. It is like the love spoken of in the monastery I visited in the desert of Egypt, "the single requirement is that he should have sensed in his heart, even though it be only once, a feeling of love for God." If I go with that love, remembered from childhood, I come to a great love, and the only thing that holds me back is the fear of being a fool of love. If I am willing to be a fool of love, I can become wise in love. I pass from a love that is unfelt, unhoped, and unwilled, to a love that lives in feeling and in hope and in willingness. I become able to love at last.

4

The Peaceable Kingdom

———

I wonder what sort of a tale we've fallen into? . . . Don't the great
tales never end?

—J. R. R. Tolkien

It is one thing to find the way to the kindling of my own
heart. It is another to "rekindle hearts in a world that grows chill,"[1]
as Tolkien says, to find what Simone Weil calls "a method of
breathing inspiration into a people." According to her, the process depends on two "word functions," on articulating "hidden
thoughts" that are capable of becoming convictions that "bring
about an inner transformation," and on speaking to "hidden needs"
with words that "infuse comfort, energy and as it were food."[2]
These two word functions are performed, I believe, by stories
that live in people's hearts and by sayings that are the moral of
stories.

What are these "hidden thoughts"? What are these "hidden
needs"? They have to do with "habits of the heart," as Alexis de
Tocqueville calls them, among us Americans with "individualism
and commitment in American life,"[3] as Robert Bellah has argued.
They have to do with the emergence and separation of the individual from humanity. There is, I would say, a double emergence: first that of humanity, an emergence which is also a separation from nature, even from God, according to traditional
stories, and then that of the individual, an emergence which is
also a separation from humanity, the loneliness that appears in
latter-day stories. The emergence is a step forward, but the separation seems to call for a reunion. Thus there are four cycles of
story. "In the first cycle, before there was night and Heaven and
Earth were separated, all animals, including humans, could speak
to one another at will," David Guss says. "There were no bar-
riers. No fear. No death." This is the primordial stage, an un-

71

differentiated unity. "With the second cycle came the first division, sometimes said to be the result of god giving birth." It was the time of the emergence and separation of humanity from nature. "The third cycle is our own, the one of the present moment." It is the time of the emergence and separation of the individual from humanity, I would say. "The fourth cycle is the one to come, when all things will be reconnected once again."[4] It is the time of the reunion of the individual with humanity, and of humanity with God, the time of universal reconciliation.

It is this final cycle of story, the peaceable kingdom described by Isaiah where "The wolf shall dwell with the lamb, and the leopard shall lie down with the kid, and the calf and the lion and the fatling together, and a little child shall lead them,"[5] that is the happy ending of the entire story of stories. It contains the moral of the story, calling me to love God with all my heart and soul and to love my neighbor as myself, to move toward the reintegration of humanity with God, that is, and of the individual with humanity. It is not the same as the first cycle, nevertheless, for it is a differentiated rather than an undifferentiated unity. The emergence of humanity and of the individual is not taken away, I mean, in the union or reunion. I am living in the light of emergence and in the shadow of separation, in the tension of "individualism and commitment," but my road, as is said in *Dark Night of the Soul,* is "the road of the union of love with God."[6]

I have to pass through the shadow of separation, "the dark night of the soul," to come to the reunion of all in God, for it is when I feel the separation that I long for the union. All the cycles, though, revolve around the same center, whether it be with centrifugal or with centripetal motion. All of them look back to the primal or forward to the ultimate One. Let us see what it would be to go through the cycles of story, to live through the centrifugal experience of emergence and separation and pass over into the centripetal experience of union and reunion.

"The heart desires too much"

Just as there is a beginning and an ending of a story, so also there is a story of the beginning and of the ending. Every story has a beginning and an ending, but the story of the beginning and of the ending is the larger sort of story that is called a myth. There is a key to myth, according to this, in every story, for instance in the story of a life. If I tell the story of my life, I may have to tell something of the larger story in which it is situated, like Geronimo beginning his story with the Apache story of creation, or Augustine ending his with the biblical story of creation. My emergence as an individual has to be placed in the larger context of the emergence of humanity. At the same time my own emergence is a key to that of humanity, and my own separation, to its separation. Sometimes we think we are in one story when actually we are in another.[7] Kierkegaard, for instance, thought of his life as a sacrificial struggle against nature, but in reality, according to Theodore Adorno,[8] it was a following out of his nature and his melancholy. The separation can conceal the emergence, I gather, and make it look like sacrifice.

I wonder if the same is true for me, if the loneliness of separation is concealing from me the true story which is one of emergence and reunion. As I meditate on Adorno's critique, however, I begin to suspect that he does not see the emergence at all. He sees only a would-be separation that fails to break with nature. I want to follow the clues in another direction, to discover the emergence concealed beneath the separation. For me Kierkegaard is a symbol of all that is deepest in individualism. The question for me then is *What becomes of the individual in our reunion with humanity and with God?* I want to consider the emergence of humanity as a rise of human feeling and that of the individual as one of personal feeling. What becomes of personal feeling, I want to ask, in our reunion with humanity, of human feeling in our reunion with God?

Immediacy with others, immediacy with God, that is our starting point in life, then a rising sense of time, a sense of having our own lives, our own journeys, that separate us from one another and from God, but then again an immediacy with others when they touch us, an immediacy with God when God touches us along our journeys, an immediacy that points to a timeless unity. "The transcendence of longing,"[9] Adorno argues, the fact that longing always reaches beyond the state we are in, means

that the longed-for state of union or reunion is never an existing
reality. "The heart desires too much,"[10] as Hölderlin says. If longing becomes love, though, as I have been saying, then union or
reunion is a real experience. It is as real as the experience of
timelessness, and that is something that is experienced at significant moments in a life. The primordial oneness from which
we come is timeless, our emergence and our separation is in time,
but we also meet one another in time, we even meet God in time,
and so there is timelessness in time, and it points to the ultimate
oneness to which we go. The primal and the ultimate One is
"mythical," but that only means it belongs to the larger story we
are in, no less true for being a story.

What then is the story I am in, if it is not simply a story
of separation and of loneliness, "a way a lone a last a loved a long
the . . ."?[11] What is the larger story that is implied in our encounters with one another and with God in time? Let us follow
"the transcendence of longing" through emergence and separation, through the long day and night of story, and see if it is taking us to a place that we already know in our hearts.

"Life is a dream,"[12] Calderón's saying, *la vida es sueño,* suggests that the story of emergence and separation is a story of
awakening. Or if there is no awakening, there is no emergence
and separation. Sometimes when we are dreaming we realize we
are in a dream. That is the way it is in Calderón's play, *Life Is
a Dream:* we awaken when we realize we are dreaming—our
awakening consists in that realization. Segismundo, a prince, has
been imprisoned all his life by his father, the king, brought up
in a lonely prison among the rocks, because according to the
stars he is to be a violent man. As it is, he has become violent
from living in chains. Then one day his father has him drugged
and brought to the palace and told when he awakens that he is
the prince. He turns out to be just as violent, though, as the stars
had foretold. So he is told that it was all a dream, and when he
awakens again he is back in his prison. Then he is freed in a
popular uprising by those who want him rather than a foreign
prince to succeed his father. But now, convinced as he is that
life is but a dream, he is no longer a violent man. Instead he

proves to be a magnanimous prince, able even to forgive his father for imprisoning him.

I am like Segismundo in prison as long as I think of myself as trapped in my loneliness, but I become like Segismundo the prince when I realize I am in a story of emergence and reunion. The moral of the story is to realize life is but a dream. There is a false emergence, according to the story, a false dawn as it were, if I try to take what is mine, like Segismundo unbound and violent. There is a true emergence, true dawn following false dawn, when I receive what is mine, like Segismundo freed and magnanimous, instead of taking it by force. What makes the difference is realizing life is a dream, realizing the story I am in is a story, that is, and letting go thus of everyone and everything in the story. As long as I hold on, I can be violent. When I let go, I can be magnanimous.

It is true, when life is said to be a dream, the meaning is that life is *like* a dream. Where is the likeness? It is in the things of life entering and passing in life, I believe, just as they enter and pass in a dream. Thus Segismundo becomes convinced that life is a dream after being prince for a day. Before that day he was only a prisoner living in his lonely prison among the rocks, and after that day he found himself again a prisoner. Being a prince had entered his life and then passed again as in a dream. So when he is freed at last and becomes a prince in earnest, he is still aware that being a prince is something transitory, something entering his life that must pass again in its time. Aware of its passage, he is able to let go of it and of all the power and glory of it. He is able to receive it rather than take hold of it by force, and as he receives it he is able to hold it loosely enough to let go of it again, and to let go also of the woman he wanted, Rosaura, and to receive the woman who is given to him by circumstances, Estrella, to receive what is given and not to take what is not given.

My life begins in dreaming, according to this, in things entering and passing, and it moves toward awakening, toward giving and receiving, when I realize things are entering and passing. There is a dangerous pass, though, between dreaming and awakening in life where I can become caught up in trying to take what is mine or what I think is mine by force or, failing that, where I can become convinced I am trapped in isolation and there is no hope. Still, I feel the longing to come into my own. "The expression for such a longing is anxiety," Kierkegaard says, "for the state out of which he longs to be proclaims itself in anxiety, and it proclaims itself because the longing alone is not sufficient to save him."[13] Someone or something has to come to meet my longing if I am to make it through this pass. Someone or something has to be there for me.

"Where the danger lies," Hölderlin says, "there likewise lies the salvation." There is danger there in the lonely pass from dreaming to awakening in life, but there is also salvation. The danger has to do with God being near and yet far, near and yet difficult to grasp. Here are the opening lines of the poem "Patmos" where Hölderlin speaks of danger and salvation:

> Near, near and
> Difficult to grasp is the Almighty.
> Yet where the danger lies, there
> Likewise lies the salvation.
> In darkness dwell
> The eagles; fearless the sons
> Of the Alps pass over the abyss
> On delicate bridges.[14]

When I feel lonely, I can feel far from God, not knowing where God is or what God wants, and yet at the same time feel close to God, as if loneliness itself, the feeling of separation, brought God near. It is my longing in my loneliness that enables me to recognize my salvation, to recognize whoever or whatever is there for me. I recognize it in the images of beauty in my life, as my longing carries me from one person to another, from one enthusiasm to another. To awaken is to remember the dream, to realize things are entering and passing, persons are coming and going, enthusiasms are rising and falling. So to awaken is to let go of the persons, of the enthusiasms, to let them save me by pointing beyond themselves.

It is in crossing the abyss "on delicate bridges" from the persons and enthusiasms of my life to God that the danger lies. For Hölderlin himself the danger was insanity, something he had encountered already in his life when he wrote these lines, crossing over and being unable to get back again to himself. He prays

> O give us wings, for the faithful
> Voyage and the return![15]

The danger is really twofold. I can be trapped on this side of the abyss, trapped in my loneliness — it is like waking from sleep but being unable to recall what I was dreaming. Then the persons and enthusiasms do not point beyond themselves, and I find myself trying in vain to wrest my salvation from them. Or I can become trapped like Hölderlin on the other side, my back turned to life, unable to turn again to the persons and enthusiasms of my life.

Salvation then is in crossing over and coming back again to myself. I cross over when I am carried out of myself and my familiar world, like Hölderlin in this poem, carried out of himself to Patmos, the place of revelation, where Saint John received the revelations of the Apocalypse. I am carried out of myself when I am caught up in a reality greater than myself, communing with God or with nature, when I open the imagination of my heart to the greater life and let it flow in upon me and express itself in my thoughts and words and deeds. I come back again to myself then when I acknowledge my own responsibility, my own choice, in my relationship to that life and that reality, when I acknowledge my thoughts and words and deeds as my own. My crossing over comes of the transcendence of longing, of its reaching beyond the things of my life, but my coming back comes of its immanence, of its rootedness in my own being. "If, as Kierkegaard writes, longing alone is not sufficient for salvation," Adorno says, "still the images of beauty devolve upon longing through which the course of deliverance, disappearing, must travel if it is ever to lead to landing and awakening."[16] By coming back to myself, I let the course of deliverance travel back through the images of beauty in my life, the persons, the enthusiasms, disappearing under their imagery and their beauty like an underground stream.

If I let the images of beauty in my life be images, if I let them point beyond themselves, then the course of deliverance becomes the same for me as the restless movement of desire, not just a movement from one image to another, but a crossing over and a return, a crossing over to God, that is, and a return to myself and to my own life. I am caught up in the movement of desire as in a stream, flowing from one thing to another, as I go from image to image, flowing above ground whenever I cross over to God, flowing underground whenever I come back again to myself and to the things of my life. Why? If it is a course of deliverance, what am I being delivered from? "The solitude of time" (*der Einsamkeit der Zeit*).[17] That is the phrase Hölderlin uses in his hymn "To Nature." In our separation from nature we have fallen into the solitude of time, where we move from one thing to another. To redeem time we must cross over and return.

"O give us wings, for the faithful voyage and the return!" Hölderlin's prayer, leads us into a story of crossing over and return where separation is turned into emergence. It leads us into a story like *A Night in the Forest* by Blaise Cendrars, "First Fragment of an Autobiography," as he calls it, which he begins with a funeral chant of the Bekairis Indians, "If your drafts of oblivion are as potent as were your kisses, enter here, for I live among the huts of the dead, where no man ever makes his way."[18] There is a forgetting in crossing over, a letting go of your life and the things of your life, like "drafts of oblivion," in order to enter into a larger reality. It takes you beyond your life, as if into the realm of death. If I were to become stranded there, I would have to say "I live among the huts of the dead, where no man ever makes his way." I would become like Hölderlin in his years of madness. He had actually crossed over the mountains to become a private tutor to a family in Bordeaux, but then he had come home again over the mountains on foot, empty-handed and lost in a kind of mild insanity. Coming back is what Cendrars' story is ultimately about. He comes back to Paris from Brazil, and is about to leave again for Spain. He spends his time in Paris remembering and meeting again. The night in the forest is a return from forgetting to remembering, from death to life.

It is by spending a night in the forest, as it were, that I come as an individual to participate in the emergence and awakening of humanity. It is like the night in the forest that young men spent in Arthurian legend to prepare for knighthood, or the "vision quest" that native Americans underwent to find spiritual power and to learn the identity of their guardian spirit. It is an exposure to danger and at the same time to salvation. If the salvation does not come from where the danger is, Heidegger comments on Hölderlin's words,[19] then it is not true salvation. It is the distance we have to cross in crossing over to God, though, that is the danger according to Hölderlin. It is the same distance we have to travel in returning to ourselves. Still, God is near, as he says. His own crossing over, at least in "Patmos," is to Christ. He seeks to come near Christ, like John the beloved disciple, "lying close to the breast of Jesus."[20]

If I cross over like this, if I let the Gospel of John speak to my heart, I may see Christ as Hölderlin saw him, "and his friends beheld him at the end, as he gazed in triumph, happiest of all."[21] I may be drawn to this happiness, drawn into it. I may come upon the danger André Malraux saw, reading the Gospel of John as he lay wounded, that "all faith dissolves life into the eternal."[22] I have to come back then to life, to dissolve the eternal into life, to bring that happiness back with me into my life. Somehow happiness is found in transcending "the solitude of time," the loneliness you feel, for instance, when you have to decide your way at a crossroads in life. "Decision time always makes me realize how alone I am in this world," a friend once wrote to me. "All of a sudden it's down to me to interpret events and meanings and reach inside myself to find truth. Why does God feel so far away at these times?" I am happy when I feel God is near, when I feel the presence of the eternal. How shall I bring happiness with me into the sense of time? How decide the course of my life in time while living in the presence?

If I realize "life is a dream," the things of life are entering, I mean, and passing, if I see death coming, as Christ did, "his spacious soul filled with a calm foreboding,"²³ as Hölderlin says, then life dissolves into the eternal for me, I see all things must pass, but the eternal also dissolves into life, I see the eternal in us and I am able to make my choice. I see what matters and what does not matter. I choose to live for God in us, for the eternal in us, to live as if the eternal mattered in us. I see time not as a solitude but as "a changing image of eternity" and the images of beauty as changing images of the eternal life. Hölderlin could see the madness coming in his life, the darkness, and yet afterwards in the dark years he could write,

> The lines of life differ,
> they are like ways, and like the confines of the mountains,
> what we are here, a God knows how to fulfill yonder
> with harmonies and everlasting requital and peace.²⁴

Here is the dilemma of the emerging individual, of emerging humanity, "the heart desires too much," as Hölderlin had written in "Evening Fantasy." We awaken to time and to the solitude of time, but we desire timeless happiness, we desire eternity. Still, there is peace already when I pass from "the unmediated vision,"²⁵ as it is called, where time is a solitude, to a vision of mediation, where time is "a changing image of eternity,"²⁶ a medium, as it were, through which eternity shines. It is a matter of light and shadow, walls and space. As long as time is opaque to eternity, I seem to be living in shadow, surrounded by walls. Time appears to be the limit of all life, the horizon of all hope. When time becomes translucent to the light of eternity, however, it seems things are meant, there are signs, the heart speaks, there is a way. And when time becomes transparent, the meaning of things, of signs, the speaking of the heart, the way becomes clear. The narrowness of time gives way to the spaciousness of eternity. What seemed too much for the heart to desire now seems too little. I am heart-whole.

As long as time for me is opaque to eternity, I seem to myself to be in a story that is not my own, "I seem to be living in someone else's story," as a friend once said to me, a story that seems to require a sacrifice of the heart's desire. It is because in time there are roads taken and roads not taken. I am haunted, as I walk alone on my chosen road in life, by the roads I have not taken, and especially it may be by some one road I almost took, by someone or something that could have been part or more a part of my life. I have to let go of someone or something, it seems, that is part of my heart's desire. If I go one step further, however, and let go also of whoever and whatever is there for me on the road I have taken, if I let go of everyone and everything, that is, then everyone and everything that enters into my life seems to be a gift rather than a theft or an exchange.

"If you are ready to leave father and mother, brother and sister, and wife and child and friends, and never see them again," Thoreau says in his little essay on walking, "if you have paid your debts, and made your will, and settled all your affairs, and are a free man, then you are ready for a walk."[27] If I am taking someone or something from someone else to make my life, I am not ready. My life to me is a theft. If I am giving up someone or something only to find someone or something else, I am not ready. My life to me is an exchange. But if I am letting go of everyone and everything, I am ready. My life to me is a gift. I walk then into the woods, into the unknown; I walk alone and yet unalone; I walk with God. For everyone and everything I encounter seems to belong to my life, to point me on my way, to speak to my heart. I blaze my trail, leaving "blazes" on the trees, entries in my journal, markings in my memory, and yet I also discover it, step by step, from the encounters, the clues, the speaking of the heart, as if my path were already laid before my feet, a way I have chosen and yet a way destined for me.

My path is my own. My story is my own. There is no visible harmony among the paths of life, among the stories people live in, as long as time is opaque to eternity, as long as time is a solitude. The only community we have then is that all hearts dwell in the same solitude, the same wilderness. We are alone then and cannot make one another unalone except by our compassion for one another, by our sharing of our loneliness. "The lines of life differ," as Hölderlin wrote, "they are like ways, and

like the confines of the mountains." As long as time is opaque
for us, we can only hope "what we are here, a God knows how
to fulfill yonder," as he said, "with harmonies and everlasting re-
quital and peace." But if time becomes translucent for us, if eternity shines through, we can find a harmony, a peace that exists
in the here and now.

"The hidden harmony is better . . ."

It is a harmony among stories people live in or among stories
that live in people's hearts, a harmony that is hidden under dissonance, under the conflict of good and evil. "And, as with all
retold tales that are in people's hearts," John Steinbeck says, "there
are only good and bad things and black and white things and
good and evil things and no in-between anywhere."[28] It is not
an in-between but an underlying unity, not the unity of a cause,
for that unifies people only by setting them against other people,
but the unity of a human being who is the subject of a story.
Or it is like that, only the unity of all human beings. It is the
eternal in us, "the indestructible" in us, as Kafka calls it. "The
indestructible is one: it is every human being individually and
at the same time all human beings collectively," he says; "hence
the marvelous indissoluble alliance of humanity."[29] It is not even
destroyed in us by evil or by the conflict of good and evil. The
mysterious thing about it is that "the indestructible is one," that
it is one and all. Our stories are various, "the lines of life differ . . . ," and yet they are one, the story of one.

"There is one story and one story only," Robert Graves says,
"that will prove worth your telling."[30] He may mean the unique
personal story. He may mean the archetypal story that is partly
enacted or reenacted in each human story. There is one story,
though, in a more comprehensive sense than either of these, a
story of which all stories are episodes. It is the larger human story,
the great journey in time of which all human journeys are a part.
It is as if all roads led into one road. "He used to say there was
only one Road: that it was like a great river: its springs were at
every doorstep, and every path was its tributary," Tolkien writes

in one of his stories. "It's a dangerous business, going out of your door, he used to say. You step into the Road, and if you don't keep your feet, there is no knowing where you might be swept off to."[31]

My life and every life, according to this, leads into a great adventure, a great journey in which we all share. Yet each life story can be told from more than one standpoint, for instance that of Christ told variously by Matthew, Mark, Luke, and John. There is an underlying unity here, a "harmony of the gospels," that is a key to the unity of all stories. "The hidden harmony," Heraclitus says, "is better than the visible."[32] I first came upon that saying when I was reading Père Lagrange on the harmony of the gospels. Now, many years later, it occurs to me that it may be true of all life stories or that the gospels in their hidden harmony may point to a hidden harmony of all life stories. It is a hidden rather than a visible harmony, the visible having disappeared in the multiplication of standpoints. It is a harmony that comes to light in passing over from one standpoint to another, in taking one standpoint and then shifting to another and letting one's vision refocus. It comes to light, but never fully, for the passing over is never finished.

"As I continued along the Way," Dag Hammarskjold says, "I learned, step by step, word by word, that behind every saying in the Gospels stands *one* man and *one* man's experience."[33] Or is it rather *many* and the experience of *many* in relation to *one?* What do I learn if I continue along the way of passing over into the stories of others and coming back again and again with new insight to my own story? Do I find the one somehow in the many?

Instead of the dream of life I find "the dream of the dream," as Paul Celan calls it, the story of the story. "I am supposed to tell you some of the words I heard deep down in the sea where there is so much silence and so much happens," he says. "I cut my way through the objects and objections of reality and stood before the sea's mirror surface. I had to wait until it burst open and allowed me to enter the huge crystal of the inner world."[34] He is speaking of passing over into the paintings of Edgar Jené, but what he says seems true of all passing over. There is a plunge

into depths like deep sea where there is silence, where things happen, where I can hear words. I have to cut my way through walls
of reality, for when I pass over I am going from what is real for
me to what is surreal, like the surrealism of Jené's paintings, where
things are joined together that are put asunder, and things are
put asunder that are joined together in reality. I come to stand
before a mirror where I am reflected and I have to wait until
it bursts open and allows me to pass into the world of the other,
an inner world like that of a crystal.

What then is "the dream of the dream"? What is the story
of the story? There is a hint in the title of one of the paintings,
A Sail Leaves an Eye. It is the story of a voyage, a journey, a parting, a separation of a sail from an eye. There is a sail in the eye,
the image of the sail on the retina, and there is another sail outside the eye, sailing away. "*A Sail Leaves an Eye.* One sail only?
No, I see two. But the first one, which still bears the colour of
the eye, cannot proceed," Celan comments. "I know it must come
back. Arduous, this return."[35] There is a parting and a return:
a sail leaves an eye on a voyage but comes back again to the eye.
Or one leaves and another returns. It is the story of emergence
and separation, I think, that ends in return and reunion, the basic
cycle of story. Only it says the parting is from an eye and the
return is to an eye. Whose eye? The human eye or the eye of God?

"There is a dream dreaming us," a Bushman hunter once
told Laurens van der Post, when asked for a story of the beginning. "But you see, it is very difficult," he said, "for always there
is a dream dreaming us."[36] We are in the dream, in the story,
and so it is difficult for us to recount the dream, to tell the story.
It is the dreaming eye that gives unity to the dream, the storytell-
ing eye that gives unity to the story, not just because the one
eye sees the many things but because the many, like the sail, leave
the eye and return to the eye. It is because the eye is included
that it is not just a dream but the dream of a dream, not just
a story but the story of a story. It is not just a seeing but the
seeing of a seeing. It is a hidden unity, a hidden harmony, as
long as the eye is not included, but here in this painting of a
sail leaving an eye it is revealed, the eye is named and depicted,

an "empty, yet strangely seeing socket" on the cliff in the background, "a fiery eye" on the sail in the foreground. It is the mind's eye, or "the mind's I," the thinker in the thought, the dreamer in the dream, the teller in the story.

If I say with Calderón "life is a dream" or really "life is dream" (*la vida es sueño* not *la vida es un sueño*), or with Shakespeare "We are such stuff as dreams are made on, and our little life is rounded with a sleep,"[37] I am not denying the eternal in us, but I am speaking of the relativity of time. I am speaking to the terrible loneliness we feel if we believe time to be the ultimate reality. If I allow the relativity of time, the "changing image of eternity," I can perceive "the dream of the dream," the story of the story, but realizing I am in the dream, in the story, I realize I am not the dreamer, not the storyteller, though I too can recount the dream, I too can tell the story. It is rather for me to listen to God telling the story or first to listen. As the man who listens to the fireflies tells the storyteller in Mario Vargas Llosa's tale, *The Storyteller* (*El Hablador*, "The Talker"), "Listen, listen, storyteller."

Listening to God, listening to the eternal in us, can indeed be like listening to fireflies:

> Silent, motionless, serene, my eyes shut, waiting. I listened but I heard nothing. At last, one night, after many nights, it happened. Over there, now. Sounds different from the sounds of the forest when night falls. Do you hear them? Murmurs, whispers, laments. A cascade of soft voices. Whirlpools of voices, voices colliding, intermingling, voices you can barely hear. Listen, listen, storyteller.[38]

It is like listening to many human voices, or listening to "the voice of many waters."[39] It is very true, "Near, near and difficult to grasp is the Almighty," as Hölderlin said, or in a later version of the same poem, "God is full of goodness, but no one can grasp God alone."[40] I cannot grasp God by myself. I have to be carried beyond myself, as Hölderlin was, carried beyond my familiar world into a larger world. There I hear "the voice of many waters," the voices of everyone and everything, but in the many I hear the one: "it is every human being individually and at the same time all human beings collectively" and yet "the indestructible is one." I listen until I hear a harmony, until I pass from dissonance to consonance, and that harmony, that consonance is what I count as insight, as if the heart of the universe were speaking in the murmurs, whispers, laments of all hearts.

What harmony can there be in "whirlpools of voices, voices colliding, intermingling, voices you can barely hear"? Not a harmony that is familiar but a harmony I have to learn, like that of twelve-tone music. Still, learning is remembering, here too, for the murmurs, whispers, laments of other hearts speak to my heart and I discover in them the murmurs, whispers, laments of my own heart. All twelve tones of chromatic music are known to me already, but never, until I hear it, in their chromatic harmony. It comes through as dissonance rather than harmony at first. It is only if I listen to it, only if I sustain my attention, that it begins to seem a harmony. So it is too with the matters of the heart. The harmony is hidden at first and comes to be revealed only if I sustain my attention, for "attention is the natural prayer of the soul."[41]

Say I pay attention, say I let heart speak to heart. I perceive our separation from one another, let us say, before I perceive our union. I perceive the dissonance of our hearts before I perceive their harmony. I enter the night of the soul before the day. "And no bridge is from man to man,"[42] Walter Calé wrote in a poem at the outset of the twentieth century. "It is impossible to experience what another person, even the nighest one, experiences on others," Franz Rosenzweig comments, though "one understands what the other says."[43] As long as I remain in my own standpoint, as long as I live only there, I cannot experience what another person is experiencing, even the nearest other. If I can pass over, though, from my own standpoint to that of another, if I can enter into the other's standpoint, I can enter into the feeling, the imagining, the thinking, the suffering of the other, I do believe. I am able to participate, I mean, in the life of the other, to commune with the other. It is true, I do not become the other, I remain myself, but I find a way to the other.

"I find something as immaterial as language, yet earthly, terrestrial, in the shape of a circle which, via both poles, rejoins itself and on the way serenely crosses even the tropics," Celan says, "I find . . . a *meridian*."[44] I find "the connective," he says, that "leads to encounters." It is as if humanity were circled like the earth by meridians, longitudinal circles passing through the north and south poles, passing through all the latitudes, passing through the equator. Each meridian is a direction, as love is a direction, that leads from one human being to another, but in a circular form that reminds me of the great circle of love that is "from God and of God and towards God." Each one is a line along which we pass over to one another and come back again to ourselves, arising from our participation in a common humanity.

"And the bridge is love," the answer to the verse, "And no bridge is from man to man," raises Julia Kristeva's questions, "Do we speak of the same thing when we speak of love? And of which thing?"[45] The answer is always a story of love. If I pass over into stories of love and come back again and again to my own story, I do find a meridian that passes through all the stories. Longing becomes love, I have been saying, but if I give longing the name Eros, the word for love in Plato, and if I give love the name Agape, the word for love in the New Testament, I am connecting the stories of Eros and the stories of Agape. What is more, the link between the two comes to light, namely, friendship or Philia. I think of the story that is told at the end of the Gospel of John, using two different words for love, the verb corresponding to Agape and that corresponding to Philia. "Do you love me?" Christ asks Peter, speaking of Agape. "Yes, Lord; you know I love you," Peter answers, speaking of Philia, as if to say "Yes, Lord; you know I am your friend." Again Christ asks and again Peter answers. And then on the third time Christ asks "Do you love me?" speaking of Philia, as if to say "Are you my friend?" Then Peter is very upset and says "Lord, you know everything; you know I love you," that is, "you know I am your friend."[46]

We go from longing to love by way of friendship, I gather, as in this story which ends with Christ saying "Follow me" and foretelling how Peter one day will lay down his life, will love, that is, with the great love. The meaning of love changes as we pass along the meridian, from longing to friendship to love, but the circle rejoins itself and love is the beginning as well as the end. "In the beginning was love,"[47] Kristeva says. I want to say that too, only I will mean by it not only that expressions of affect are the most primitive language, cries and exclamations that come before any proper words, but that being loved comes before loving. Inarticulate affects and the sense of being loved go together, however, as love in memory, coming before understanding and willing love, as what we know of love before we understand it and willingly choose it.

As I go from memory to understanding to will, I emerge as an individual. As I go backward in recollection from will to understanding to memory, I recover my roots, I go back to the matrix from which I have emerged, but I also go forward towards a reunion with humanity and with God. I go back towards being loved; I go forward towards loving. "One is attracted precisely to the extent that one is neglected,"[48] Michel Foucault says, and it is true, the loneliness of my life measures the depth of my longing, and yet my sense of being loved is what enables me to go on from just longing to being a friend and being a lover. If "attention is the natural prayer of the soul," it is attention as a kind of prayer that carries me back to my roots to discover a sense of being loved: "I am, therefore I am known and loved,"[49] and it is attention that carries me forward along the meridian from love to love, from being loved to loving. Attention finds love even in longing: the depth of my loneliness becomes the depth of my sense of being loved; the intensity of my longing becomes the intensity of my loving.

"The poem is lonely," Celan says. "It is lonely and *en route.*" I am lonely. I am lonely and *en route.* Does this not place me, as he says it places the poem, "in the encounter, *in the mystery of encounter?*"[50] There is mystery in the encounter of one human being with another, once the individual has emerged from humanity and become separate, once the individual is lonely. What is the mystery? It is in our reunion with humanity and with God. We already share in a common humanity, and that is the basis of human society. Our common humanity, though, the human essence, is our capacity for knowledge and love. The reunion is the realization of our capacity, its unfolding in actual knowing and loving, something more, therefore, than the bare existence of human society. It is an awakening to the capacity itself and to our sharing it, like learning to speak.

Or better, since "I speak" has become a paradox for us, as Foucault says, much as "I lie" was for the ancient Greeks,[51] it is more like learning to say "I." It is by emerging fully as an individual that I come to a reunion with humanity and with God, I am thinking, by completing again and again the movement of passing over to others and coming back to myself. For it is when I come back to myself that I come back to humanity and to God. I think of a story Celan tells about meeting a friend in the mountains. In real life, he says, he missed meeting the friend and instead encountered himself. But in the story he has himself meeting his friend and groping through conversation to the point where he can meet himself and say "I." The last sentence is striking: "me here, me, who can tell you all this, could have and don't and didn't tell you . . . me, maybe accompanied—now—by the love of those I didn't love, me on the way to myself, up here," or in another translation, "I here, I: I who can tell you all, who could have told you; I who will not tell you and have not told you . . . I perhaps accompanied—at last!—by the love of those unloved, I on the way to myself, up here."[52]

There is a parable here of meeting another, of meeting oneself, of meeting no one, of meeting God. I think also of Celan's Psalms to No One. Here as there he calls out to "No One." He says "Do you hear me?" He is like the Marquis of Bolibar crying "Do you hear me, Lord?"[53] He is resolving the paradox of "I speak," saying "I speak" is empty if there is no one to speak to, if there is no God, but it begins to have meaning if I begin to speak to No One, if I begin to pray. "I listen," on the one hand, has meaning already because if I listen, I am paying attention, and "attention is the natural prayer of the soul." Listening takes me directly into prayer, speaking is empty unless it becomes praying, and learning to say "I" is learning to say "thou," learning to speak and to listen to the eternal "thou."

Learning to say "I," therefore, does not mean coming to a universal "I," coming to a oneness in which there is "no more Thou in the I,"[54] as Buber had once thought, but coming, as he later believed, to the oneness of "I and thou." The unity is a relational unity. When I come to myself, I am accompanied, "maybe accompanied — now — by the love of those I didn't love" or "by the love of those unloved." I have gone from a condition of walking alone, unloved as it seemed and unloving, to one of walking with others, loved and loving. But I have come to it by realizing that the previous state was not true to life, that in fact I was loved when I thought I was unloved, that I loved even or was *in* love without knowing it when I thought I did not love. My realizing it, nevertheless, makes a great difference. My emergence as an individual came not so much of walking alone as of willingness to walk alone, a willingness that welcomes companionship rather than a will to walk alone that rejects companions. When I realize then that I have companions, I come home to myself.

Thus learning to say "I" speaks also to the ancient paradox "I lie" (if it's false, it's true, and if it's true, it's false). For learning to say "I" is learning to speak the truth. Gollum, the liar in Tolkien's story, almost never says "I," and when he does there is a suspicion that he is telling the truth.[55] In fact, the ancient paradox was not originally formulated as "I lie." Rather it was Epimenides the Cretan saying "All Cretans are liars" or really "Cretans are always liars, evil beasts, lazy gluttons."[56] When it is formulated as "I lie," the hidden paradox comes to light,

(a) as if saying "I" revealed the paradox,
(b) as if saying "I" revealed the truth,
(c) as if it were paradoxical to lie and say "I."

It is by saying "I," accordingly, that Jesus reveals the truth in the Gospel of John, saying "I am" to pronounce the Word that he is, saying "it is I" to answer the quest of the human heart that always seems to desire too much, saying "I" to reveal the hidden harmony of "I in them and thou in me." I can still say "I," therefore, in our reunion with humanity and with God. Indeed *it is by truly saying "I" that I enter into the human reunion, into the union of love with God.* "I" is the password. For I am an inscape into humanity, an inscape into God. When I listen for the hidden harmony, for the resonance in my own heart with the hearts of others, with the heart of the universe, I hear at first what seems a discord rather than a concord. "Wherever we are, what we hear is mostly noise," the composer John Cage says, "When we ignore it, it disturbs us. When we listen to it, we find it fascinating."[57] If I continue to listen, I do find it fascinating, I hear the harmony, I am drawn into it, as if my heart were beating in a rhythm with the heart of God.

5

The Sense of "I" in Christianity

The word "I" is the true shibboleth of humanity. So listen to this word!

— Martin Buber

"I'm alive!" There is a moment in Ray Bradbury's story *Dandelion Wine* when the boy who is the main character realizes "I'm alive."[1] He is wrestling with his brother, rolling over and over in the woods, when he stops, dazed with the wonder of it. His brother says "Are you all right?" But he gives a great soundless shout inside himself, "I'm alive! I'm really alive!"

There is indeed a wonder, even a mystery about the sense of "I," and it plays a role in Christianity. That is what I want to go into here. I had originally thought to write about "an endless conversation"[2] of faith and faith, of faith and reason, of faith and conscience. As I was working on it, my sister suggested that I use actual conversations. So I wrote down three conversations I had, brief exchanges really, one with David Daube, one with René Girard, and one with Erik Erikson. I found all three had to do with the sense of "I" in Christianity. And so it has become my theme here. I have come to realize that the sense of "I" is the locus of peace. I borrow the phrase, "the sense of 'I,'" from Erik Erikson. In each of these conversations it is I who ask and the other who answers, and in each of them I am left pondering the answer. I include here not only the conversations but also my ponderings, and I come in the end to a kind of formula for the sense of "I."

Before I come to the conversations, let me make two introductory remarks. I will try to define two senses of "I" in Christianity. One links "I" with will. Self and will emerge together in a life, it seems, as when a little child just learning to talk says "No" and "mine." "No" expresses will, "mine" expresses self. When I think of this, I always think how long a journey it is from "No" and "mine" to "Yes" and "yours." I think of the long journey Dag Hammarskjold came to say "For all that has been—Thanks! To all that shall be—Yes."[3] When Michel Foucault, studying "technologies of the self," as he calls them, speaks of "the renunciation of one's own will and of one's own self"[4] in Christianity, he is speaking of this journey. It is not a destruction of will, I think, but a movement from will to willingness that leads us into our own center, the other and more fundamental sense of "I."

"We all have within us a center of stillness surrounded by silence,"[5] Hammarskjold says. This is the more fundamental sense of "I," our center, the quiet place within us. It is a hollow center. Thus when someone attempts to tell the story of a personal conversion, the story often proves to have "a hollow core."[6] The before and the after come out in the story but the actual moment itself remains elusive. It is as if the sense of "I," at least in the stories we tell, comes out to be a kind of zero point where all things meet. "I never had, and still do not have, the perception of feeling my personal identity," Claude Levi-Strauss says in the Introduction to *Myth and Meaning*. "I appear to myself as the place where something is going on, but there is no 'I,' no 'me.' Each of us," he goes on to say, "is a kind of crossroads where things happen."[7] I am reminded, as I ponder his words, of the Buddhist doctrine of "no self." At the same time, it occurs to me that the sense of "I" in Christianity may be something very similar to this, a place where something is going on, the place in us where God comes to dwell. That phrase in Hammarskjold's formula is a clue, "surrounded by silence." When I am in my own center, I am surrounded by a silence that is a presence, the very presence of God. If I may use a somewhat risky metaphor, I will say it is like standing inside a hollow tree, one of the giant redwood trees in the Muir Woods, surrounded on all sides by a living being (I know what Freud would say of this!). Now we are ready for the three conversations.

"I am": A Conversation with David Daube

I will begin with a conversation I had some years ago with David Daube on the "I am" sayings of Jesus. It was a conversation of faith and faith, I can see now, a meeting of two types of faith, Jewish and Christian, not exactly the "two types of faith"[8] that Martin Buber speaks of, faith in someone and faith in something, I and thou and I and it, but two ways of faith in someone, of I and thou. I had not read David's work at that time on *The New Testament and Rabbinic Judaism* where there is a chapter on "The 'I am' of the Messianic Presence."[9] As it turned out, he did not simply repeat to me what he had already said there but put the whole thing in a rather more personal way. His work is essentially "Essays in New Testament Judaism"[10] as he subtitles a recent book. His faith appears in his way of understanding the immediacy of Jesus with God. It is a Jewish sense of immediacy, but it helped me to understand the Christian sense of mediation.

Here is the gist of our conversation:

D.D.: Jesus in the perspective of the New Testament is "He that Cometh," a prophet, a messiah, even *the* Messiah. You have to realize, though, that to say he is God is something that sticks in a Jew's throat. The strongest statements of that kind in the New Testament are the "I am" sayings, not "I am" with a predicate following such as "the way, the truth, and the life," but "I am" without any further predicate. In these sayings Jesus is echoing the "I am" of the burning bush or the "I am and no other" of the Passover liturgy.

J.D.: But do you believe that Jesus really said these sayings? Don't most scholars regard them as later expressions of faith?

D.D.: I believe they are *ipsissima verba,* his own very words! But when he said "I am" he was not saying "*I* am," pointing to himself, I think, but "I am," pointing to the divine presence, to the Shekinah, the presence of God in him and through him. Consider, for instance, the passage in Mark where the disciples are in the boat and he says to them "Don't be afraid, I am" (not merely "It is I" as in the translations) or the passage in John where he meets the soldiers in the garden and says "I am" (not merely "I am he" as in the translations) and they fall to the ground.

J.D.: I see what you mean. It makes sense, and it seems likely enough that Jesus will have said "I am" and meant it that way, as if to say "God is here," or as you put it (in the lecture "He that Cometh"), "The Divine Majesty itself is here."[11]

I am Glaucon in this conversation, and David is Socrates, and I end up like Glaucon saying "Now I understand, Socrates." Yet as I think it over afterward I see that something more could be said. It is true, the awareness of Jesus seems focused on the presence of God, and this thought that Jesus is referring to the presence, the Shekinah, seems a real clue to the actual consciousness of Jesus. His awareness is, as Buber says, an "immediacy toward God."[12] It has been suggested in recent work on the historical Jesus that "the message of Jesus was a proclamation of the unmediated presence of God," that his gospel was one of "divine immediacy and human immediacy."[13] On the other hand, it does seem the translators are right, the "I am" of divine presence does come through to his hearers as "It is I" and "I am he," Jesus becomes to his disciples the mediator of the divine presence. Thus we are led into the mystery of the incarnation, that God is present to us in him and through him. Still, we are invited into his immediacy ourselves, into "immediacy toward God" or, as Buber also says, into "unconditional relation"[14] with God.

God is near and far when there is nothing human between you and God, "so near and yet so far"[15] as Tennyson says, near because there is nothing to separate you, far because there is nothing to join you. I can pass over to the standpoint of Jesus, I believe, enter into his relation with God. But I have also to come back again to myself, to make his God my God. This is mediation, as I understand it, to enter into his immediacy and to come back again to my own immediacy, my own "so near and yet so far."

"I will die": A Conversation with René Girard

Passing over to Christ and coming back to myself is like Christ taking my place and me taking his. Can Christ take our place? Can we take his? That is the matter at issue underlying my second conversation, one with René Girard, who has proposed "a non-sacrificial reading of the Gospel text."[16] Instead of the "substitutionary atonement" where Christ undergoes the death due to our sins, Girard has it that Christ is the victim who reveals the innocence of all victims and the violence of human society. I see the shunning of any doctrine of exchange or of substitution as linked with the feeling expressed in Martin Heidegger's formula, "No one can take the Other's dying away from him."[17] It is the conviction that we each have our own death to die. Just as "I am" is the fundamental certainty in the thinking that comes from Descartes, so "I will die" is the fundamental certainty in the thinking that comes from Heidegger. I feel the force of "I will die" but I also feel the force of "one died for all,"[18] and I think of our conversation thus as one of faith and reason.

There has always been a blind spot, it seems, in doctrines of substitution: If Jesus takes our place in death, what is the significance of his resurrection from the dead? I find something of the same blind spot in Girard's thinking where Jesus, instead of substituting, reveals the substitution that is going on in desire and in violence. The resurrection seems to point to something else, not just that Jesus takes our place or shows how victims take our place but that we take his place, that we go with him through death to life.

Here is the brief interchange we had, my question and Girard's answer:

J.D.: In your thinking, as I understand it, Jesus is the victim who reveals the innocence of all victims and the violence of human society. That is the significance of his death, but what is the significance of his resurrection? Doesn't his resurrection imply that there is more to his death than that?

R.G.: The resurrection is a mystery of faith. I don't mean to explain the mysteries, but only to affirm what can be affirmed of Jesus "in a rational light."[19] As Simone Weil says, "The mysteries of faith are degraded if they are made into an object of affirmation or negation, when in reality they should be an object of contemplation."[20]

We went on afterward to have a panel discussion on Simone Weil, but we never got back to her idea of the mysteries of faith. As I thought about it later, it seemed to me the death of Jesus is a mystery too, one and the same mystery as his resurrection.

Indeed the Christian mystery here is that of passing through death to life, his passage and ours. The more I thought of it, nevertheless, the more it seemed to me that Girard is onto something here, the substitution that is going on in desire, how we want what we see others want, and in violence, how we do unto others as has been done unto us. When it comes to Jesus then, it seems clear as he says that Jesus is not simply a substitute, a scapegoat for our sins, but is one who reveals our sin, our violence and how it is always finding a scapegoat. The mission of Jesus thus, as in the Gospel of John, is "to bear witness to the truth."[21] Still, the truth he reveals, I believe, is not just the innocence of all victims and the violence of human society. It is the truth of the unconditional love of God, the truth of the love that is stronger than death, stronger than violence. It is revealed thus not in his death by itself but in his passage through death to life. I think Girard would agree, only he would say the innocence of all victims and the violence of human society is accessible to reason here while the love that overcomes death, that overcomes violence is accessible only to faith.

What then of the matter in issue, "I will die"? Is it true to say, as Heidegger does, "No one can take the Other's dying away from him"? If we say "one died for all," and understand that by way of substitution, we still have our own death to die. "Of course someone can 'go to his death for another,'" Heidegger says. "But that always means to sacrifice oneself for the Other 'in some definite affair.'"[22] If we go deeper into the mystery of exchange, however, and understand "one died for all" by way of participation, then the sense of "I" is transfigured. Just as the loneliness of "I am" is touched by the "I am" of divine presence, so the loneliness of "I will die" is touched by the sense of passing with Christ through death to life. It becomes a loneliness that is consciously shared, if that is still loneliness, a sense of being caught up in eternal life.

The Sense of "I": A Conversation with Erik Erikson

All the loneliness in the basic human certainties, "I am" and "I will die," is overshadowed in faith by "I am with you." It is a vision of life pervaded by hope. There is a link between hope and the sense of "I," according to Erik Erikson; "hope connotes the most basic quality of 'I'-ness," he says, "without which life could not begin or meaningfully end." Speaking of the life cycle now from the standpoint of old age, he sees life as a journey from "basic trust," the life task of earliest childhood, to "faith," as he says in *The Life Cycle Completed,* "the last possible form of hope matured."[23] Although he comes from a Freudian background, he deliberately uses the word "I" instead of the word "ego," and he connects the sense of "I" more with hope than with will. Self linked with will is changed, renounced, transfigured, I want to say too, as we go the long journey from "No" and "mine" to "Yes" and "yours," from will to willingness, as we enter into the stance of Christ toward death, "not as I will, but as thou wilt."[24] Self linked with hope, on the other hand, is abiding, as in the saying "hope springs eternal."

Linked with hope, the sense of "I" is like "the inner light" of which the Quakers speak, "the light within," or even "the Christ within." That is the way Erikson seems to think of it in his late works, using phrases like "the shining light."[25] In fact, after his work on Luther and on Gandhi he has become fascinated in his late years with the sense of "I" in the sayings of Jesus. It was after a talk he gave on "the Galilean sayings and the sense of 'I'"[26] before a small group of us at Cape Cod that I had a brief conversation with him on the "I" sayings of Jesus.

I begin with something he said in the talk about the Golden Rule (which didn't appear afterward in the published version of the talk) and then add my question and his answer:

E.E.: The Golden Rule in most traditions is negative, "Do not unto others what you would not wish them to do unto you," but is affirmative in the sayings of Jesus, "Do unto others what you would have them do unto you." Thus Jesus characteristically leads us into ourselves, into our own inwardness, to discover what we truly desire. This inwardness is the sense of "I" pervading all his Galilean sayings.

J.D.: When Jesus says "I am," do you think he means the Shekinah, the presence of God in him and through him, as David Daube says, or do you think he means himself and his own inwardness?

E.E.: I think the "I am" is both personal and transcendent.

I thought at first he was saying something equivalent to the Christian doctrine of Jesus as a person with a divine and a human nature. Afterward, reading the written version of his talk where he speaks of "individuality and universality,"[27] I thought he was saying rather that the "I" of which Jesus is speaking is both personal and universal, personal because Jesus is speaking from the heart, universal because he is speaking to the heart. Now, as I think it over again, I can see also how he could use the word "transcendent." God speaks when the heart speaks, the voice of conscience is the voice of God, as Gandhi is always saying, and thus the "I am" expressing that voice is at once personal as coming from conscience and transcendent as coming from God. That is why I think of our conversation now as one of faith and conscience. "I" as Jesus says it, and even "I am" as Jesus says it, is something we can say too, according to this, something Jesus is teaching us to say, just as he teaches us to say "Our Father. . . ." I am reminded of Meister Eckhart saying whatever is true of Christ is true also of us. To say there is something unique, something incommunicable about Jesus and his sense of "I" puts a distance between us and him.

Still, I want to say there is something unique, something incommunicable. We cross the distance, it is true, when we pass over to Jesus, but it is there again when we come back to ourselves. There is both intimacy and distance in passing over and coming back. What we come to is participation. When we step into his relation with God, he vanishes from in front of us, and yet he is still there dwelling within us, as Paul says, "that Christ may dwell in your hearts by faith."[28] In fact, it is we who vanish in the end and he who is there, "I live; yet not I, but Christ lives in me."[29]

"Christ dwells in you as you"

It is a moment of wonder in a life when one comes to realize "I am," like the twelve-year-old boy in Ray Bradbury's story when he realizes "I'm alive." It is another such moment when one comes to realize "I will die," when one's life opens up before one all the

way to death, when no one else can take one's death away and
one realizes one must die it oneself. And it is still another such
moment when the loneliness of "I am" and "I will die" is overshadowed by "I am with you," when one comes to realize "Christ
dwells in you as you," if I may paraphrase the Hindu formula,
"God dwells in you as you."[30] At each of these moments we are
carried back to the same place within ourselves, "a center of stillness surrounded by silence." There are words here that break
the silence, "I am," "I'm alive," "I will die," "I am with you," "Christ
dwells in you," "God dwells in you." Yet all the formulas lead us
back into the silence that surrounds our center of stillness. The
endless conversation does end after all in silence.

We pass over to one another, I mean, we pass over even
to Christ, but we come back again to ourselves. When we pass
over, things seem luminous and communicable. When we come
back again to ourselves, things seem mysterious and incommunicable, each person a mystery, and Christ the central mystery
of all. Our conversation ends in the silence of mystery. Thus my
conversation with David Daube ends in the mystery of the divine presence, "I am and no other," and my own thoughts afterward end in the mystery of the incarnation, "I am" with the force
of "It is I" and "I am he." My conversation with René Girard
ends in the mystery of the resurrection, Jesus alive and living
in us, and my own thoughts afterward in that of our own passage
with him through death to life, "I am with you." My conversation with Erik Erikson ends in the mystery of "the inner light,"
"the light within," "the Christ within," and my own thoughts afterward in the mysteriousness of this light, like Chesterton's "terrible crystal," "more mysterious than darkness."[31]

All these mysteries, it seems, are one mystery. Running
through all three conversations is the thought of indwelling, of
God's presence in Christ, of Christ's presence in us, as in the
formula in the Gospel of John. "I in them and thou in me."[32]
I think of Martin Buber on "I and thou" where the sense of "I"
depends on the sense of "thou." What I have found in these conversations is something more complex, not just relationship, "I
and thou," but also indwelling, "in them" and "in me." The sense

of "I" in Christianity, I conclude, has a bright pole, that of relationship, and a dark pole, that of indwelling. What came out in the conversation with David Daube is "I am" meaning "thou in me," God in Christ; in that with René Girard "I will die" overshadowed by "I in them," Christ in us; in that with Erik Erikson the link between "I in them" and "thou in me," the inner light in us and the everlasting light in Christ. Instead of substitution pure and simple, Christ taking our place, I have come to an idea of participation where he disappears in us, where we disappear in him, where he is in us and we are in him.

Christ dwells in you as you. That is the formula I come to for the sense of "I" in Christianity. It is parallel to the Hindu formula, "God dwells in you as you," but it is also perpendicular to it. For if I say "Christ" here rather than "God," I leave intact the personal relationship, the "I and thou," of the human being with God, and thus also the sense of a personal God, and yet I affirm at the same time the indwelling, the union or oneness with God. What I am saying then is that Christ is the ownmost self of the Christian. It is true, we find in Christianity the same hollow center we find in Buddhism, "a center of stillness surrounded by silence," but it is filled with grace, with grace that comes through the void. Each center is unique, but because of the grace flowing through it is one with every other center. As a friend once said to me of that other formula, "God dwells in you as you," it cuts right through the deep loneliness that seems to isolate us from one another. There is indeed a loneliness that is not taken away by good community bonds, nor even by the intimate relationship of one human being with another. Yet the indwelling presence reaches even that deep, touches even that loneliness. It links every human island to the main.

6

The Peace of the Present

a presence in the present
—Paul Celan

Inscribed on the gate of a mosque in the ruined city of Fatehpur-Sikri, south of Delhi in India, are the words, "Jesus (peace be upon him) said: The world is a bridge. Pass over it, but do not build your house on it."[1] For me the saying rings true, the ruins seem to verify it. We pass over to one another, we pass over to God, but we always come back again to ourselves and to God in us. So we don't make our home on the bridge but come home to ourselves and to God dwelling within us. We come to the eternal in us, to the peace of the present, to a presence in the present.

It is true, if we do not pass over the bridge of the world, if we do not pass over the bridge of love, we are never able to come home, never able to be at home with ourselves and with God. We experience only the restless longing for home. By following "the meridian," as Celan calls it, the great circle that circles the earth, that leads from one human being to another, we come back again to ourselves, our starting point, and become like a poem, "a presence in the present." A poem, he says, is "one person's language become shape and, essentially, a presence in the present."[2] I follow the meridian by passing over to other persons and coming back ever and again to myself, and as I do so, my language become shape, I enter into communion and communication. I am *incommunicado*, without means of communication, in solitary confinement, until my life becomes a journey, until I begin crossing "the bridge of sighs" that goes from heart to heart. That is the meaning of the saying, "The world is a bridge," I believe, life is a journey in time, a journey that leads us into the far places of the heart.

There are "places in the heart which do not yet exist," Leon Bloy says, "and into them enters suffering that they may have existence."[3] There are places, he is saying, where we do not yet feel, and there are places that are numb, where we no longer feel, and into these places suffering comes, the suffering of lack and of loss, the suffering of love, and then there is feeling where there was no feeling, and these places in the heart come into evident existence. Also they come to light when I pass over to another person and enter into the other's feelings. I come back then to myself and feel the resonance of feeling within my own heart, feeling in sympathy or in empathy with the heart of the other. And as I continue my journey, as I pass over not only to other persons but also to other cultures and other religions, coming back always to myself and to my own, I enter more and more into a "heart to heart" relation with others. (A young Trappist monk from Indonesia told me the phrase "heart to heart" exists also in his language, *hati ke hati*). I come closer to the heart of all.

Am I able, simply by living in this way, to "work the peace of the present"? "If you can command these elements to silence and work the peace of the present," the boatswain says in *The Tempest*, "we will not hand a rope more." Am I able, simply by walking the unviolent way of passing over to others and coming back to myself, to live in the peace of the present? Yes, I want to say, I am able to live in the peaceful eye of the storm and to move with it, following the path of the storm.

It is in going to the heart of all, I mean, by entering our own center of stillness, that we come to be a presence in the present. We find there in our center "the end of desire," as I have called it, the fulfillment of what we desire, only we find the end again and again, coming back to it from one thing after another, as if it were an endless end. Story can lead desire to climax in violence, it has been said, but desire left to itself turns every climax into an anticlimax as it moves ever on from one thing to another.[4] Desire is fulfilled, I want to say, but in peace rather than in violence. To say that, though, I have to draw a distinction between "mimetic desire" and "heart's desire," between desiring what we see others desiring and desiring what we truly desire. Story can give expression to heart's desire as well as to mimetic desire, can lead towards a fulfillment in peace as well as towards a climax in violence. Desire moves on, but it comes back again and again to rest in our center of stillness. The restlessness of desire is expressed in passing over to one person after another, the rest in coming home to ourselves.

A rest in restlessness, the thing we come to here, seems to be an acceptance of the whole process of passing over and coming back, a sense that "the road goes ever on,"[5] as Tolkien says, a thought very akin to "the world is a bridge." If I accept the restlessness of my own heart, if I go with it, I enter, consenting, into the process of passing over to one person after another and I find rest in coming back each time to myself. But I find an enduring peace in my acceptance of the journey itself, of the road going on, of the bridge of the world. My center of stillness thus becomes a moving center, like the moving eye of a hurricane, moving along the path of the journey. I am able not only to come to peace again and again, but actually to live in peace.

It is thus that the end of desire is also "the beginning of desire." The expression "heart's desire" is ambiguous, meaning both the desiring and the desired of the heart, the one the beginning, the other the end of desire, but the two are one, the desiring and the desired, when I realize what it is I desire, to know and be known, to love and be loved, to be caught up in love, even in the love of God, and in the awareness, the knowledge that it brings, when I realize "God is my desire," as Tolstoy said. For then I know there is always more to know than I know, more to love than I love. So I am always setting out. At the same time I know I am known and loved already beyond all measure. So I am always coming home. The world of the heart's desire is round, I am always coming home, always setting out, my beginning is in my end and my end is in my beginning. My circling the earth, following the meridian from one human being to another, passing over to the other, coming back to myself, is what I have been calling "contemplation," a unity of poetry and thought, a unity of thinking and thanking, a unity of all life in prayer.

"Attention is the natural prayer of the soul," the saying of Malebranche, taken up by Walter Benjamin and Simone Weil and Paul Celan, is the key here to the nature of contemplation. It means paying attention to the things that happen and to the persons who enter my life, persons from my own times, figures also from past times, paying attention to the signs of my life and of my times and to the promptings of my heart, and thus finding my way. It means paying attention to God in others, to God in me. Thus it is truly "the natural prayer of the soul." Violence arises, it seems, where contemplation is absent, in a life without contemplation, in a society without the contemplative life.

"Why is there anything at all, rather than nothing?"[6] the riddle of existence, is answered by the love of God, I believe; "I am, therefore I am known and loved." Or, more in the form of "I think, therefore I am," I can say "I am known and loved, therefore I am." When the riddle is not a riddle, when there is no contemplation, the existence of things is no wonder, is taken for granted. Violence arises in that lack of feeling and awareness. What is more, it numbs the heart, it takes feeling and awareness away. A friend, a veteran of the war in Vietnam, once showed me something he had written in a diary while in combat, describing an action in which many were killed. "You see," he said, "I wasn't feeling anything." There is feeling, there is awareness in violence, to be sure, but there is no feeling for the wonder of life, no awareness of the mystery of existence. Or violence takes that feeling, that awareness away. That is why violence is mimetic, it seems, why we do unto others as has been done unto us. It is because we have feeling only for likeness, for doing as has been done, because we have no feeling for presence, for the mystery of living and dying.

Numbing and being numbed, the cause and effect of violence, is undone in recollection. If we come to feeling through recollection, like my friend who said "You see, I wasn't feeling anything," we pass from a violent to an unviolent way. Here it is not so much "emotion recollected in tranquillity"[7] as numbness recollected that becomes emotion in being recollected, in tranquillity, indeed in the peace of the present. What was violence becomes peace in being recollected, not that it is a false recollection, but the recollection of violence is peaceful rather than violent, like the "war music" of *The Iliad* and of the Gita and of *War and Peace.* We pass from a violent to an unviolent way in that recollection is the first step on the way to understanding and to unviolent will.

I find this structure in Shakespeare's *Tempest:* memory, understanding, and will. Only Prospero, who has worked the storm by his magic, is able to "command these elements to silence and work the peace of the present." He has engulfed his enemies in a magical storm, and only he can free them. First he recalls the past, telling the story of his exile to his daughter and getting her to remember as much as she can. "What seest thou else in the dark backward and abysm of time?" he asks her, but she can remember little of her childhood, and what she can see is "rather like a dream than an assurance."[8] Then he comes to an understanding of his enemies, feeling for them in their present troubles. "If you now beheld them, your affections would become tender," Ariel, his helping spirit, tells him. "Dost thou think so, spirit?" Prospero returns. "Mine would, sir, were I human," Ariel says. "And mine shall,"[9] Prospero agrees. Then finally he forgives his enemies, his will toward them becomes unviolent, and all ends well, but part of his unviolent will is to give up his magical power, "This rough magic I here abjure,"[10] and this leaves him powerless and dependent upon mercy. "Now my charms are all o'erthrown, and what strength I have's mine own, which is most faint," he says in the epilogue, ". . . and my ending is despair unless I be relieved by prayer, which pierces so that it assaults Mercy itself and frees all faults."[11]

Where there is understanding there is forgiveness, and where will is unviolent there is renunciation of the use of force. Still, there is human reciprocity. "As you from crimes would pardoned be," Prospero concludes, "let your indulgence set me free." Just as violence is mimetic, we do unto others as has been done unto us, so nonviolence is "heart to heart," we release and are released. So Prospero, forgiving his enemies, hopes in turn to be released from exile. Strength is personal, Hannah Arendt says, force is impersonal, but power is interpersonal.[12] Nonviolence is often the use of power against force, as in a general strike. What I am saying, though, is when nonviolence breaks with the mutuality of violence, it begins a new mutuality, not power maybe but still an interpersonal link where "heart speaks to heart" and "nation shall speak peace unto nation."[13]

"Do unto others as they have done unto you," the rule of mimetic violence, and "Do unto others as you would have them do unto you,"[14] the Golden Rule, differ by "as you would have them." They differ, that is, by the heart's desire, by its absence or its presence. When it is absent, I have to wait on its presence, to wait on love, to go through memory to understanding and will.

> Come unto these yellow sands,
> And then take hands,[15]

Ariel sings, allaying the fury of the storm and the sorrow of the prince, who thinks he has lost his father the king in the shipwreck, and leading the prince to Prospero's daughter and to love. I have first to "come unto these yellow sands," to turn from the sea to the shore, to come into the peaceful eye of the storm, the tranquillity where emotion can be recollected, "and then take hands" by entering into relationship with the things of my life, with the persons who belong to my life, letting them be and opening myself to their mystery. Then I am able to discover love in my life, even a great love, in the form of loneliness, of longing, of heart's desire.

It is true, I have still to be faithful to love, to be faithful to my heart's desire. There is a movement from faithfulness to faith, just as a countermovement is possible from betrayal of love to despair. Sometimes the word "love" is restricted to mean faithful love or even more narrowly to mean love in faith, but I want to use it also to mean the love of longing, a love that can still be present in betrayal, though betrayal lived out leads ultimately to numbness and lack of all feeling of love. If I am faithful to my heart's desire, following it and letting it decide the road I take, I come to faith, seeing light with my heart even when my eyes see only darkness. If I forsake it, betraying the great love of my life, I come instead to despair, seeing only darkness with my heart when my eyes see darkness, seeing only with my eyes.

What is the great love of my life? To claim to be one of the friends of God or one of the lovers of God can seem too much, but to say with Tolstoy "God is my desire" is to speak simply of the love of longing. I too can say "God is my desire." There is a sea-change that takes place in love, as in death:

> Full fathom five thy father lies;
>   Of his bones are coral made;
> Those are pearls that were his eyes;
>   Nothing of him that doth fade
>   But doth suffer a sea-change
>   Into something rich and strange,[16]

Ariel sings to the prince, singing of death, but it is true also of love. If I follow my heart's desire, I go through a sea-change myself. There is a direction in the restless movement of desire, though desire may seem to have no direction, going from one thing to another. It is the direction of love. If I am faithful to my heart, the direction becomes more apparent, becomes conscious and willing, for I have to let go of things, one after another, as desire carries me on, and open myself to the mystery that is showing itself and yet hiding itself in the things of desire in my life.

Mystery, showing and hiding itself in persons, in things, is what love is about. I am being drawn into a mysterious life. If I follow the trail of mystery, I become like an artist. "In order to paint one has to go by the way one does not know," Milton Avery said. "Art is like turning corners; one never knows what is around the corner until one has made the turn."[17] Life too is like turning corners, I want to say, and in order to live I have to go by the way I do not know. I am led by life into the unknown but on a road that other roads join, a road that "goes ever on and on," a road on which I become ever more pure and simple, as Avery did in his painting. For mystery is the one in the many, God in us, the wonder that pervades our lives. Love and death are sea-changes then "into something rich and strange," as I walk the road into mystery, for I am walking "the road of the union of love with God."

I am in a story of which I do not know the ending, though

I say "the union of love with God," for I am at a midpoint where
humanity has emerged, where I have emerged and I feel the loneliness of separation, where the reunion with humanity and with
God is still to be consummated. I do not know what will become
of me in love and in death until I have tasted love, until I have
tasted death. I have already a foretaste, to be sure, and I speak
of "the union of love," but in saying this I am looking into "the
dark backward and abysm of time" where we were one, according to story, and into the dark forward and abysm of eternity
where we shall again be one but consciously and willingly. I am
coming to consciousness and willingness, going by the way I
do not know, turning corners, never knowing what is around
the corner until I have made the turn. "Still round the corner
there may wait a new road or a secret gate," as Tolkien says, "and
though I oft have passed them by, a day will come at last when
I shall take the hidden paths that run west of the moon, east of
the sun."[18]

Each time I pass over to another person, I come back to
myself to find "a new road or a secret gate" in my own life, things
that were there all along "though I oft have passed them by." Even
if I pass over to ordinary people and situations, much as Avery
in his painting chose simple and ordinary subjects, I come back
to myself to find something essential. "I strip the design to the
essentials," Avery said; "the facts do not interest me so much as
the essence of nature."[19] It is that essential nature that I discover
in others and then in myself that becomes "a new road" for me
"or a secret gate," for it is the eternal in us, the infinite in us.
It is our inexhaustible capacity for knowledge and love, a capacity
that becomes a call, like the voice of the wind, leading us on "the
hidden paths that run west of the moon, east of the sun," the
paths of the eternal, the paths of the infinite.

"East of the sun and west of the moon"[20] is a phrase from
a Norwegian folktale about a girl who travels east of the sun and
west of the moon to free her beloved prince from a magic spell.
The kingdom that is east of the sun and west of the moon is the
land of heart's desire. It is so far away that she must seek help
of the north wind to carry her there, so far away that it seems

"the heart desires too much," and yet she does succeed in reaching it, and when she arrives she rescues the prince, using the help she has been given by her guides along the way. There is a freeing of the heart, a rescuing of the person, that has to take place, I gather, if you are ever to dwell in the land of heart's desire. It is necessary to break the spell, to realize "life is a dream," the things of life are entering and passing as in a dream, if you are ever to become heart-free and heart-whole. "The way to that kingdom is hard," a storyteller concludes, "but if you reach it, you will find a welcome within."[21] It is hard to follow the heart by letting go of the things of life, but you will find a welcome within, a welcome that goes from heart to heart.

"We are such stuff as dreams are made on," Prospero says when he is coming to the point of letting go of his powers, though he is disturbed by his lack of control over life, by his failure to change Caliban's ugliness of mind. "A turn or two I'll walk to still my beating mind," he says. "We wish your peace,"[22] his daughter and her prince say as they leave him. And peace is what he comes to and what we come to if we follow him. "East of the sun and west of the moon" is certainly such stuff as dreams are made on, but the point of the story is to break the magic spell and thus to realize the heart's desire. To give up the powers of magic is similar. It is to give up control over the things of life. Instead of giving up wish-fulfillment, as Freud thought, it means fulfilling our strongest desire, our central wish, that in us which stirs our inmost being. It means sounding the hidden harmony of souls.

Here is the turn that leads into the kingdom. If we have emerged as the human race, separate from the rest of creation, if I have emerged as an individual, separate from the rest of humanity, then the kingdom is in our reunion with one another and with God, and the first step in reunion begins from the last step in emergence, the sense of "I." There is a giving up of self and will in giving up control over the things of life, in letting myself be led by God, by the illumining of my mind and the kindling of my heart. The sense of "I" changes as I pass from will and control to letting be and openness to mystery, as I pass from will to willingness. My sense of "I," once located in my will, comes to be located in the center of my being, "a center of stillness surrounded by silence." Coming to my own center, I come into touch with other centers as well. It is as though we were living in an infinite sphere where the center is everywhere and the circumference is nowhere, the infinite sphere of God's presence.[23] My sense of "I" becomes thus "a new road or a secret gate" into the kingdom of God.

"Loss of self"[24] is a description that has been given to Alzheimer's disease. I wonder if the loss is of the self that is linked with will, leaving intact the deeper self that is linked with the center of one's being. That would be a hopeful possibility. Anyway it is one thing to lose control and another to let go of control. The one is an unwilling loss of will, the other a willing release that leaves will intact in the form of willingness. "Not as I will, but as thou wilt" speaks of that letting go, "I am" speaks out of the center. If I too can say "not as I will, but as thou wilt," then I too can say "I am" out of the center of my being. When Jesus says "I am" in the Gospels, he is speaking, it seems, of the Shekinah, the presence of God, he is speaking out of the silence surrounding the center of stillness. The presence of God is the surrounding silence.

When I say "I will die," on the other hand, when I say it with anxious foreboding, that is, and not yet with peaceful acceptance, I am speaking of the self that is linked with will, the self that meets a horizon limiting all its projects, the horizon of time and death. "No one can take the Other's dying away from him," Heidegger's saying, is true of this self linked with will. I have to die my own death. It is not true, it seems, of the deeper self linked with the center of my being. "I am the resurrection and the life," Jesus says in the Gospel of John; "he who believes in me, though he die, yet shall he live, and whoever lives and believes in me shall never die."[25] I am a center of stillness surrounded by silence, and here the silence speaks, becomes word, and the word is "I am," and it calls me also to say "I am," and to say it in the face of "I will die." In the infinite sphere of God's presence the center is everywhere and always and the circumference is nowhere and never. My identity at this deep center is not as lonely and separate as it is on the level of will. It is here I find union with God and with humanity. The center that is everywhere is at my center.

"Christ dwells in you as you," as I understand it, means just that, the center that is everywhere is at your center. A center that is everywhere is divine, as God is everywhere, but as your center or as my center it is human, the center of a human being. And the distinction remains between the human center and the divine encompassing, the still center of the human being and the surrounding silence of the divine presence, the human "I" and the divine "thou." So the sense of "I" is not lost in reunion with God and with humanity. There is still the human center and the human willingness to be in the center of stillness, to be surrounded by the divine silence. We are alone, surrounded by silence, and yet unalone, surrounded by presence.

Once, when I was a child ten years old, I had the experience of being in the eye of a hurricane. It has become for me now a kind of image of life. There were several of us children staying at the summer home of some friends of our family on Houston Bay. The adults had all gone into the city when the hurricane struck, a late summer storm on the Gulf of Mexico. A hurricane is a tropical cyclone, a system of winds rotating around a center of low pressure, the eye of the hurricane, where there are only light winds or even complete calm and sometimes sunlit clear sky. One edge of the rotating circle was moving seaward, the other shoreward. It was the edge moving seaward that struck first, blowing down some trees and driving the water far out. Then came the calm as we passed into the eye. We children, knowing nothing about hurricanes, thought the storm was over, and someone said "Let's go swimming!" So we all ran down from the house and out into the water. There was complete calm, but the sky was dark and growing darker. Then someone said "It's getting scary!" And so we all ran in again. Then the other edge of the storm struck, driving in towards shore. We went down into the bottom of the house, as the electricity had gone out, and gathered around a lantern and told ghost stories. I remember lamplit faces as we sat there in a circle, scaring fear away.

Living in the peace of the present is like living in the eye of a hurricane. It means living in "a center of stillness surrounded by silence," the center we all have within us, and moving with the center as it moves with time. For if we stop moving, we are caught by the moving edge of the storm. "The war machine is exterior to the State apparatus," it has been said. "It is the invention of the nomads."[26] War, it is true, is the path of the storm, of conflict, but peace, I want to say, follows the path of the storm, lives in the eye of the storm. *It is by living life as a journey, being led by the peace of the present, out of the past and into the future, that I am able to live in peace.* War comes not of being on a journey, like the nomads, but of living off center.

Peace comes of a sense of being on an adventure in time while living in a timeless serenity. It comes of living in a center that is moving. Thus the saying, "The world is a bridge. Pass over it, but do not build your house on it." Peace comes of living as if this world and the other world were really one world, as if the whole, the eternal in us, were more than a sum of parts, as if the human figure and its divine ground could be reversed, "Not I, but God in me."[27] The sense of "I," located in the moving center of life, is the place where the other world passes through this world, where the eternal enters time in us, where the human figure emerges and then returns to its divine ground. It is a place where God comes into the world and where the world comes back to God. "I is an other," Rimbaud's deliberate solecism, *Je est un autre,* [28] is a deconstruction of the sense of "I," and it comes from outside the center, just as "I am" comes from the center. It comes from separation, just as "I am" comes from union and reunion of figure and ground. War can be only if "I is an other," peace only if "I am."

Once all was one, according to story. All living beings were able to understand each other and to live in harmony. We walked and talked with God. Then we came into our own as human beings and separated from the rest of creation. Now we have come into our own as individuals and separated also from one another. We have come to the sense of "I." We feel the loneliness, though, of our separation and look again for union, for reunion with one another and with God. It is the longing in our loneliness that leads us back together again, "a long desire"[29] that leads to every adventure. It leads us to the storm center of our lives and times. And there we find peace, at the heart of desire.

Notes

Preface

1. Shakespeare, *The Tempest,* act 1, scene 1, line 22. Stephen Orgel follows the usual reading, "the peace of the present," in the Oxford Shakespeare, *The Tempest* (Oxford: Clarendon, 1987), p. 98. Frank Kermode, following a conjecture of J. C. Maxwell, proposes to read instead "the peace of the presence" in the Arden Shakespeare, *The Tempest* (London: Methuen, 1969), p. 5 and p. 166 (additional notes).

2. J. R. R. Tolkien, *Smith of Wooton Major* and *Farmer Giles of Ham* (New York: Ballantine, 1988), p. 38.

3. I used the distinction between limited and total war in my article, "Realpolitik in the Decline of the West" in *The Review of Politics* 21 (January, 1959): 131–50.

4. I am following the spelling of Pablo Neruda in *The Heights of Macchu Picchu,* trans. Nathaniel Tarns (New York: Farrar, Straus & Giroux, 1966).

1. The Ways of Desire

1. William Butler Yeats, *Collected Plays* (New York: Macmillan, 1963), pp. 41, 43, and 47.

2. Yeats, *The Land of Heart's Desire* (London: Unwin, 1894), pp. 24 and 43.

3. Yeats, *Collected Plays,* p. 40.

4. René Girard, *Things Hidden since the Foundation of the World,* trans. Stephen Bann and Michael Metteer (Stanford, Ca.: Stanford University Press, 1987), p. 328.

5. Joel Marks, ed., *The Ways of Desire* (Chicago: Precedent, 1986), p. 15, n. 12.

6. Charles Williams, *Many Dimensions* (Grand Rapids, Mich.: Eerdmans, 1981), p. 198.

7. Dietrich Bonhoeffer, *Letters and Papers from Prison,* ed. Eberhard Bethge (New York: Macmillan, 1971), p. 234.

8. George Bernard Shaw, *Man and Superman* (London: Constable, 1930), p. 171.

9. Jean-Michel Oughourlian, *Un mime nommé désir* (Paris: Grasset, 1981).

10. J. R. R. Tolkien, *The Lord of the Rings* (London: Allen & Unwin, 1969), p. 848.

11. Jean Paul Sartre, *Being and Nothingness,* trans. Hazel E. Barnes (New York: Washington Square, 1966), p. 724. Cf. Thomas L. Shaffer, *Death, Property, and Lawyers* (New York: Dunellen, 1970), pp. 1–12.

12. Quoted by C. G. Jung in his autobiography, *Memories, Dreams, Reflections,* ed. Aniela Jaffe, trans. Richard and Clara Winston (New York: Vintage, 1963), p. 186.

13. C. S. Lewis, ed., *George MacDonald: An Anthology* (London: Bles, 1946), p. 28.

14. See Sartre's autobiography, *The Words,* trans. Bernard Frechtman (New York: Fawcett, 1966).

15. Martin Buber, *The Way of Man* (Secaucus, N.J.: Citadel, 1966), p. 18.

16. Girard, *Things Hidden since the Foundation of the World,* p. 297.

17. Charles Williams, *He Came Down from Heaven* (and *The Forgiveness of Sins*) (London: Faber & Faber, 1950), p. 25.

18. C. S. Lewis, ed., *George MacDonald,* p. 29.

19. Freud quoted by Erik Erikson in *Identity: Youth and Crisis* (New York: Norton, 1968), p. 136. See also the novel by Gwyneth Cravens, *Love and Work* (New York: Knopf, 1982), p. 286. She has a more recent novel called *Heart's Desire* (New York: Knopf, 1986)!

20. Quoted by Clara Thomas, *Love and Work Enough: The Life of Anna Jameson* (Toronto: University of Toronto Press, 1967) title page and p. 150.

21. Robert Jay Lifton, *Boundaries* (New York: Random House, 1969), pp. 21–34.

22. Martin Heidegger, *Discourse on Thinking,* trans. John M. Anderson and E. Hans Freund (New York: Harper & Row, 1966), p. 55 (I am translating *Gelassenheit* here as "letting be" instead of "releasement").

23. Yeats, *A Vision* (New York: Collier, 1966), p. 143.

24. John Howard Griffin, *Follow the Ecstasy: Thomas Merton, the Hermitage Years, 1965–1968* (Fort Worth, Tex.: Latitudes, 1983), p. 90.

25. Saint John of the Cross, *Dark Night of the Soul,* trans. E. Allison Peers (Garden City, N.Y.: Doubleday, 1959), p. 34.

26. Pablo Neruda, *The Heights of Macchu Picchu,* trans. Nathaniel Tarn (New York: Farrar, Straus & Giroux, 1966), p. 19. Parts I–V of the poem are about the modern problem of death, VI–XII about the ascent to Macchu Picchu.

27. Joseph Conrad, *Heart of Darkness* (New York: Penguin, 1978), p. 8.

28. Girard, *Things Hidden since the Foundation of the World,* p. 380.

29. Griffin, *Follow the Ecstasy,* p. 80.

30. Ibid., p. 107.

31. C. S. Lewis, ed., *George MacDonald,* pp. 98–99.

32. Thus A. D. Sertillanges, *Saint Thomas and His Work,* trans. Godfrey Anstruther (London: Blackfriars, 1957), p. 53. Elizabeth Chase Geissbuhler, *Rodin: Later Drawings* (Boston: Beacon, 1963), p. 87, has Rodin telling Bourdelle to read the word "art" for the word "God."

33. Søren Kierkegaard, *Purity of Heart Is to Will One Thing,* trans. Douglas V. Steere (New York: Harper & Row, 1965).

34. Erikson, *Identity,* p. 136.

35. Swami Muktananda, *Getting Rid of What You Haven't Got* (Oakland, Ca.: S.Y.D.A. Foundation, 1978), p. 10.

36. Ibid.

37. H.D. (= Hilda Doolittle), *Notes on Thought and Vision* (San Francisco: City Lights, 1982), p. 39.

38. Luke 24:26.

39. H.D., *loc. cit.*

40. Ralph Harper, "The Concentric Circles of Loneliness," in his *Sleeping Beauty and Other Essays* (Cambridge, Mass.: Cowley, 1985), p. 26.

41. Deuteronomy 6:5.

42. Psalm 38:9.

43. On this contrast of Eckhart and Heidegger see my *House of Wisdom* (San Francisco: Harper & Row, 1985), p. 119.

44. Maxim Gorky, *Reminiscences of Leo Nicolaevich Tolstoy,* trans. S. S. Koteliansky and Leonard Woolf (New York: Huebsch, 1920), p. 12.

45. George Steiner, *Martin Heidegger* (New York: Viking, 1979), p. 158.

46. Sanhedrin 106b. I am using *Sanhedrin* trans. Jacob Shachter and H. Friedman (London: Socino Press, 1969) in *Hebrew-English Edition of the Babylonian Talmud,* ed. I. Epstein. See also Michael Signer's use of this saying in Jakob J. Petruchowski, ed., *When Jews and Christians Meet* (New York: State University of New York Press, 1988), p. 73.

47. Philippians 4:6–7.
48. Douglas V. Steere in his biographical memoir introducing Thomas R. Kelly, *A Testament of Devotion* (New York: Harper & Row, 1941), p. 1.
49. Stephen Rogers (1933–1985) quoted by Philip Sloan in *Humanitas* 1, no. 2 (Spring 1986): 41.
50. A. N. Whitehead, *Religion in the Making* (Cleveland and New York: World, 1967), p. 151.

2. Violent and Unviolent Ways

1. On the historic link between nonviolence and negative views of the world see David Daube, "Black Hole" in *Rechtshistorisches Journal* 2 (1983): 188–89.
2. Helen Luke, "Choice in the Lord of the Rings" (an unpublished essay quoted with permission of the author), p. 3.
3. Augustine, *Homilies on I John,* VIIth Homily, in *Augustine: Later Works,* trans. John Burnaby (Philadelphia: Westminster, 1955), p. 316.
4. Christopher Logue, *War Music* (London: Jonathan Cape, 1981).
5. Mohandas K. Gandhi, *An Autobiography: The Story of My Experiments with Truth,* trans. Mahadev Desai (Boston: Beacon, 1968), pp. 469–71.
6. Ibid., p. 504 (the epilogue).
7. Ibid., p. 466.
8. See my discussion of these words in *The Reasons of the Heart* (New York: Macmillan, 1978; rpt. Notre Dame, Ind.: University of Notre Dame Press, 1979), p. 1.
9. A. N. Whitehead, *Religion in the Making* (New York: Macmillan, 1926), p. 160.
10. Augustine's discussion of the founding murder is in *The City of God,* Book XV, chapter 5. For the contemporary discussion see Robert G. Hammerton-Kelly, ed., *Violent Origins* (Stanford, Ca.: Stanford University Press, 1987) where Walter Burkert, René Girard, and Jonathan Z. Smith speak of "Ritual Killing and Cultural Formation."
11. *Hamlet,* act 3, scene 2, line 201.
12. Girard in *Violent Origins,* p. 122.
13. Matthew 13:35. I am thinking of Girard, *Things Hidden since the Foundation of the World.* See my discussion of Augustine thinking back

to the beginning in *A Search for God in Time and Memory* (New York: Macmillan, 1969; rpt. Notre Dame, Ind.: University of Notre Dame Press, 1977), pp. 55–57.

14. Gaston Bachelard as quoted by Murray Cox and Alice Theilgaard, *Mutative Metaphors in Psychotherapy* (London: Tavistock, 1987), p. xiii.

15. Augustine, *Confessions,* Book X, chapter 26. The translation I am quoting is *The Confessions of Saint Augustine,* trans. Edward Bouverie Pusey (Franklin Center, Pa.: Franklin Library, 1982), p. 209.

16. Karen Horney uses these terms in her later work, *Neurosis and Human Growth* (New York: Norton, 1950), p. 9. In her earlier work, *Our Inner Conflicts* (New York: Norton, 1945), p. 5, she uses the terms "moving against people" (mastery), "moving toward people" (love), and "moving away from people" (freedom).

17. Martin Heidegger, *An Introduction to Metaphysics,* trans. Ralph Manheim (Garden City, N.Y.: Doubleday, 1961), p. 144.

18. See my discussion of the phrase "heart speaks to heart" in *The House of Wisdom* (San Francisco: Harper & Row, 1985), p. 6. The sentence "My heart speaks clearly at last" is from J. R. R. Tolkien, *The Lord of the Rings* (London: George Allen & Unwin, 1976), p. 439.

19. I am using Randall Jarrell's translation, *Goethe's Faust* (part 1, scene 3) (New York: Farrar, Straus & Giroux, 1976), p. 61. "In the beginning was the deed" is a straightforward translation of "Im Anfang war die Tat" set over against "In the beginning was the Word," "Im Anfang war das Wort." "It's impossible to put such trust in the Word" is a very free rendering of "Ich kann das Wort so hoch unmöglich schätzen."

20. Reiner Schürmann, *Meister Eckhart* (Bloomington, Ind.: Indiana University Press, 1978), p. 105.

21. Friedrich Dürrenmatt, *The Assignment* (with the subtitle, "on the Observing of the Observer of the Observers"), trans. Joel Agee (New York: Random House, 1988), pp. 120–21.

22. Dürrenmatt, ibid., epigraph. For another translation see Søren Kierkegaard, *Either/Or,* vol. I, trans. David Swenson and Lillian Marvin Swenson (2nd ed. rev. by Howard A. Johnson) (Princeton, N.J.: Princeton University Press, 1971), p. 24. Still another translation is given in the middle of Dürrenmatt's story, pp. 70–71.

23. Hannah Arendt, *The Human Condition* (Garden City, N.Y.: Doubleday, 1959), pp. 169–71 (on consequences of action), 212–19 (on the power of forgiveness), 219–23 (on the power of promise).

24. Augustine, *Confessions,* Book VII, chapter 10 (p. 129 in Pusey's translation).

25. See my *House of Wisdom,* p. 107 (and note 32 on pp. 116–17).

26. Dürrenmatt, *The Assignment,* p. 107 and p. 109.

27. Tolkien, *The Lord of the Rings,* p. 370.

28. Simone Weil, *The Iliad or The Poem of Force,* trans. Mary McCarthy (Wallingford, Pa.: Pendle Hill, 1983), p. 25.

29. Ibid., p. 36.

30. G. F. W. Hegel, *Reason in History,* trans. Robert S. Hartman (New York: Liberal Arts Press, 1954), p. 44.

31. Goethe, *Poetry and Truth from My Own Life,* trans. R. O. Moon (Washington, D.C.: Public Affairs Press, 1949), p. 683.

32. John Briley, *Gandhi: The Screenplay* (New York: Grove Press, 1982), p. 119 (also p. 180).

33. Quoted by B. R. Nanda in *Gandhi and His Critics* (Delhi: Oxford University Press, 1985), p. 4.

34. Austin Tappan Wright, *Islandia* (New York: New American Library, 1975), p. 663.

35. Constance DeJong and Philip Glass, *Satyagraha* (New York: Standard Editions, 1980), p. 49.

36. Martin Buber, *The Way of Man,* trans. Maurice Friedman (New York: Citadel, 1966). These are the titles of the first three chapters.

37. Eugen Herrigel, *Zen and the Art of Archery* (New York: Vintage, 1971), pp. 107–8.

38. These words of Acharya Vinoba Bhave echoing the Gita are quoted by a contemporary African writer, Es'kia Mphahlele, *Renewal Time* (London: Readers International, 1988), p. 211.

39. Tagore quoted by Es'kia Mphahlele, ibid., p. 215.

40. Buber, *The Way of Man,* titles of chapters 4 and 5.

41. Ibid., title of the last chapter.

42. DeJong and Glass, *Satyagraha,* p. 57.

43. Ibid., p. 61.

44. Ibid.

45. Gandhi's formula and Khan's are compared in Eknath Easwaran's book on Khan, *A Man to Match His Mountains* (Petaluma, Ca.: Nilgiri Press, 1984), p. 11. King's formula is in *A Testament of Hope: The Essential Writings of Martin Luther King, Jr.,* ed. James M. Washington (San Francisco: Harper & Row, 1986), p. 512, and the better known passage calling for black "self affirmation" is on p. 246.

46. See my discussion of Kierkegaard's formula of self relating to

self and being "grounded transparently" in God in *The Church of the Poor Devil* (New York: Macmillan, 1982; rpt. Notre Dame, Ind.: University of Notre Dame Press, 1983), p. 127.

47. Gaston Bachelard, *Water and Dreams,* trans. Edith Farrell (Dallas, Tex.: Pegasus Foundation, 1983), p. 42.

48. Girard, *Things Hidden since the Foundation of the World,* p. 137.

49. Paul Marechal, *Dancing Madly Backwards* (with the subtitle *A Journey into God*) (New York: Crossroad, 1982), pp. xiii–xiv (on the title).

50. Goethe, *Poetry and Truth from My Own Life,* p. 684. Although his autobiography covers his life only to 1775, he wrote it in later years and almost surely had the events of 1812 in mind when he wrote this passage about "God against God."

51. Immanuel Kant, *Perpetual Peace,* ed. Lewis White Beck (New York: Bobbs-Merrill, 1957), p. 3.

52. David Daube, *Civil Disobedience in Antiquity* (Edinburgh at the University Press, 1972), pp. 84–85.

53. Tolkien, *The Lord of the Rings,* p. 739.

54. Isak Dinesen (Karen Blixen), *Anecdotes of Destiny* (New York: Vintage, 1985), pp. 155–231.

55. Isaiah 35:10.

56. João Ubaldo Ribeiro, *An Invincible Memory* (New York: Harper & Row, 1989), epigraph.

57. Paul Claudel, *Two Dramas,* trans. Wallace Fowlie (Chicago: Regnery, 1960), p. 298 (*The Tidings Brought to Mary,* act 4, scene 2). I have modified the translation of the question, using the French text in Claudel, *Theatre* (Paris: Gallimard, 1965), vol. 2, p. 214.

58. Miguel de Unamuno, *Tragic Sense of Life,* trans. J. E. Crawford Fletch (New York: Dover, 1954).

59. See David Daube, "Jonah: A Reminiscence" in *Journal of Jewish Studies* 34, no. 1 (Spring 1984): 36–43.

60. Una Ellis-Fermor as quoted by Murray Cox and Alice Theilgaard, *Mutative Metaphors in Psychotherapy* (London: Tavistock, 1987), p. 242.

61. Leo Tolstoy, *The Kingdom of God Is Within You,* trans. Aline Delano (New York: Scribner's, 1922), p. 1.

62. Ibid., p. 254.

63. S. L. Frank, ed., *A Solovyov Anthology,* trans. Natalie Duddington (Westport, Conn.: Greenwood, 1974), p. 233.

64. John 14:27.

65. Robert Jay Lifton, *Death in Life* (New York: Random House, 1967), p. 505.

66. Job 1:15, 16, 17, 19 (King James Version) and Herman Melville, *Moby Dick* (New York: New American Library, 1961), p. 513 (epilogue).

67. Marcel as quoted by Lifton, *Death in Life*, p. 507.

68. Cox and Theilgaard, *Mutative Metaphors in Psychotherapy*, pp. 98–105.

69. Meister Eckhart, *Die Deutschen Werke*, ed. Josef Quint, vol. 2 (Stuttgart: W. Kohlhammer, 1971), pp. 169 (medieval original) and 667 (modern German translation). The English translation is mine.

70. Cox and Theilgaard, *Mutative Metaphors in Psychotherapy*, p. x (these three sentences I am quoting occur here in the Acknowledgments but are used as principles all through this excellent book on the images we live in).

71. God among the Kikuyu is called both Ngai or Mogai, "the divider," and Mwene-Nyaga, "the one who shines." I learned this from a Kikuyu friend, Sister Agatha Mwangi. See these names also in Jomo Kenyatta, *Facing Mount Kenya* (London: Heinemann, 1979), pp. 3 and 234.

72. Hebrews 4:12.

73. Weil, *The Iliad or The Poem of Force*, pp. 29–30.

74. Bachelard, *The Psychoanalysis of Fire*, trans. Alan C. M. Ross (Boston: Beacon, 1964), p. 112.

75. A. G. Mojtabai, *Blessed Assurance* (Boston: Houghton Mifflin, 1986).

76. Rainer Maria Rilke, *The Notebooks of Malte Laurids Brigge*, trans. M. D. Herter-Norton (New York: Norton, 1964), p. 209.

77. Ibid., p. 212.

78. King George VI quoted these words of Minnie Louise Haskins in his Christmas broadcast of 1939, *King George VI to His Peoples, 1936–1951* (London: John Murray, 1952), p. 21.

3. Waiting on Love

1. Gandhi as quoted by Erik Erikson, *Gandhi's Truth* (New York: Norton, 1969), p. 93 (cf. p. 410).

2. Song of Solomon 2:7, 3:5, and 8:4.

3. Leo Perutz, *Leonardo's Judas*, trans. Eric Mosbacher (New York: Arcade, 1989), p. 14.

4. Ibid., p. 143.

5. Leonardo as quoted by Monica Strauss, *Leonardo da Vinci* (Mt. Vernon, N.Y.: Artist's Limited Edition, 1984), p. 5.

6. Leonardo da Vinci, *Notebooks,* ed. Irma A. Richter (New York: Oxford University Press, 1980), p. 288.

7. Ibid.

8. Martin Heidegger, *Discourse on Thinking,* a translation of *Gelassenheit* by John M. Anderson and E. Hans Freund (New York: Harper & Row, 1966), p. 62. It is Karl Jaspers who says Heidegger's philosophy is "without love" (*ohne Liebe*), quoted by Elisabeth Young-Bruehl, *Hannah Arendt, for Love of the World* (New Haven, Conn.: Yale University Press, 1982), p. 75.

9. Michel Foucault, *Technologies of the Self* (Amherst: University of Massachusetts Press, 1988), p. 13.

10. Isak Dinesen (Karen Blixen), *Last Tales* (New York: Random House, 1957), p. 100.

11. Luke 10:41–42.

12. Luke 10:39.

13. Heidegger, *Discourse on Thinking,* p. 68.

14. Ibid., p. 82 ("exulting in waiting") and p. 81 ("the highest willing").

15. I am quoting here from the pamphlet I received at the monastery, *Welcome to the Monastery of St. Macarius* (Cairo: Monastery of St. Macarius, 1983), p. 7. I assume the author is Matta el-Meskeen, the spiritual father of the monastery.

16. Perutz, *Leonardo's Judas,* p. 121.

17. Ibid., p. 146.

18. Walt Whitman, *Song of Myself,* ed. Edwin Haviland Miller (Iowa City: University of Iowa Press, 1989), p. 5 (line 121) (cf. the skeptical responses of Marki and Berryman on p. 70).

19. Giorgio Vasari, *The Life of Leonardo da Vinci,* trans. Herbert P. Horne (London: at the Sign of the Unicorn, 1903), p. 27. The first phrase Vasari is quoting from Petrarch, "Tal che l'opera fosse ritardata dal desio"—I have translated it here.

20. Leonardo, *Notebooks,* p. 217.

21. Paul Valery, *Introduction to the Method of Leonardo da Vinci,* trans. Thomas McGreevy (London: John Rodker, 1929), p. 15.

22. W. B. Yeats, *A Vision* (New York: Collier, 1966), p. 180. See my discussion of this passage in *The Reasons of the Heart,* p. 78.

23. Tolkien, *The Lord of the Rings,* p. 48.

24. Isaiah 30:15 in *The New American Bible* (Washington, D.C.: Confraternity of Christine Doctrine, 1970).

25. Simone Weil, *Waiting for God,* trans. Emma Craufurd (New York: Putnam, 1951), p. 135.

26. Perutz, *Leonardo's Judas,* p. 120.

27. Ibid., p. 144.

28. *Selected Poems by Gabriela Mistral,* trans. Doris Dana (Baltimore: Johns Hopkins University Press, 1971), pp. 16-21.

29. Weil, *Waiting for God,* p. 89.

30. Ibid.

31. Matthew 11:12 in the Douay-Rheims and Confraternity versions.

32. Flannery O'Connor, *The Violent Bear It Away* (New York: Farrar, Straus & Cudahy, 1960), pp. 113-114.

33. See my discussion of this passage in Proust in *The Reasons of the Heart,* p. 71.

34. Karl Rahner, *Theological Investigations,* vol. 4, trans. Kevin Smyth (Baltimore: Helicon, 1966), p. 58.

35. O'Connor, *The Violent Bear It Away,* p. 242.

36. "Joy without a cause" is from Meister Eckhart; "consolation without any preceding cause" is from *The Spiritual Exercises* of Saint Ignatius. See my discussion of these phrases in *The Homing Spirit* (New York: Crossroad, 1987), p. 72.

37. Matthew 26:39.

38. Rahner, *loc. cit.*

39. Perutz, *The Marquis of Bolibar,* trans. John Brownjohn (New York: Arcade, 1989), pp. 50-51.

40. Ibid., p. 53.

41. Isak Dinesen (Karen Blixen), *Out of Africa* (New York: Random House, 1938), p. 41.

42. I learned this saying, like the two names of God (see above, chapter 2, note 71) from Sister Agatha Mwangi. See the following note for Kenyatta's discussion of this saying.

43. Jomo Kenyatta, *Facing Mount Kenya,* p. 238.

44. Luke 18:4-5 and 11:8.

45. Perutz, *The Marquis of Bolibar,* p. 17.

46. Simone Weil, *Gravity and Grace,* trans. Arthur Wills (New York: Octagon, 1983), p. 55.

47. T. S. Eliot, *Four Quartets* (New York: Harcourt Brace Jovanovich, 1971), p. 28 ("East Coker," lines 123 and 126).

48. David Daube, *The New Testament and Rabbinic Judaism* (Salem, N.H.: Ayer, 1984), p. 291.

49. Paul Celan, *Last Poems,* trans. Katherine Washburn and Margret Guillemin (San Francisco: North Point Press, 1986), p. 211 (from his prose piece, "Conversation in the Mountains").

4. The Peaceable Kingdom

1. J. R. R. Tolkien, *The Lord of the Rings* (London: Allen & Unwin, 1969), p. 1122 (Appendix B).

2. Simone Weil, *The Need for Roots,* trans. Arthur Wills (New York: Octagon, 1984), p. 191.

3. Robert Bellah, *Habits of the Heart* (with the subtitle *Individualism and Commitment in American Life*) (Berkeley: University of California Press, 1985).

4. David M. Guss, *The Language of the Birds* (San Francisco: North Point, 1985), pp. xiv–xv. See my discussion of the two separations in *The Reasons of the Heart,* p. 63.

5. Isaiah 11:6.

6. Saint John of the Cross, *Dark Night of the Soul,* trans. E. Allison Peers, p. 34.

7. I owe this idea to my sister. Her most striking instance was Saint Benedict Joseph Labre who went from one monastery to another, thinking he was called to be a monk, and then after traveling all over Europe in his quest, came at last to realize he was not a monk but a pilgrim.

8. Theodore W. Adorno, *Kierkegaard,* trans. Robert Hullot-Kentor (Minneapolis: University of Minnesota Press, 1989).

9. Ibid., p. 140.

10. Hölderlin, "Evening Fantasy" in *Some Poems of Friedrich Hölderlin,* trans. Frederic Prokosch (Norfolk, Conn.: New Directions, 1943), p. 19. (The pages are not numbered in this edition, and so I have numbered them myself, starting with the title page.)

11. James Joyce's *Finnegans Wake* (New York: Viking, 1959) ends with these words "a way a lone a last a loved a long the" but begins with the next word "riverrun" so that the book makes a complete circle.

12. Pedro Calderón de la Barca, *Life Is a Dream,* trans. Edwin Honig (New York: Hill & Wang, 1970).

13. Søren Kierkegaard, *The Concept of Anxiety,* trans. Reidar Thomte and Albert B. Anderson (Princeton, N.J.: Princeton University Press, 1980), p. 58.

14. Hölderlin, "Patmos" in *Some Poems of Friedrich Hölderlin,* p. 23.

15. Ibid., p. 25.

16. Adorno, *Kierkegaard,* p. 140.

17. Hölderlin, "To Nature" in *Some Poems of Friedrich Hölderlin,* p. 3 (the German on p. 2).

18. Blaise Cendrars, *A Night in the Forest: First Fragment of an Autobiography,* trans. Margaret Kidder Ewing (Columbia: University of Missouri Press, 1985), p. 6.

19. Heidegger, *Poetry, Language, Thought,* trans. Albert Hofstadter (New York: Harper & Row, 1971), p. 118.

20. John 13:23.

21. Hölderlin, "Patmos" in *Some Poems of Friedrich Hölderlin,* p. 29.

22. André Malraux, *Anti-Memoirs,* trans. Terence Kilmartin (New York: Bantam, 1970), p. 194. See my discussion of this passage in *The Way of All the Earth* (New York: Macmillan, 1972; rpt. Notre Dame, Ind.: University of Notre Dame Press, 1978), p. 168.

23. Hölderlin, *loc. cit.* in note 21.

24. *Hölderlin,* ed. Michael Hamburger (New York: Pantheon, 1952), p. 266 (my translation).

25. Geoffrey H. Hartman, *The Unmediated Vision: An Interpretation of Wordsworth, Hopkins, Rilke, and Valéry* (New Haven, Conn.: Yale University Press, 1954).

26. Plato, *Timaeus* 37d (my translation). See my discussion of this idea in *The House of Wisdom,* p. 3 and pp. 60–68 and pp. 104–6.

27. Henry David Thoreau, *Walking* (Boston/Cambridge, Mass.: Applewood, 1987), pp. 4–5. (The pages are not numbered in this edition, and so I have numbered them myself, starting with the title page.)

28. John Steinbeck, *The Pearl* (New York: Viking, 1965), p. 2.

29. Franz Kafka, Aphorism #67 in *The Great Wall of China,* trans. Willa and Edwin Muir (New York: Schocken, 1970), p. 175. See my discussion of this aphorism in *The Reasons of the Heart,* p. 56.

30. Robert Graves, "To Juan at the Winter Solstice" in his *New Collected Poems* (Garden City, N.Y.: Doubleday, 1977), p. 105. See the discussion in Cox and Theilgaard, *Mutative Metaphors in Psychotherapy,* pp. 5–6 and 247.

31. Tolkien, *The Lord of the Rings,* p. 87.

32. Heraclitus, Fragment #47 in *Heraclitus of Ephesus,* ed. I. Bywater, trans. G. T. W. Patrick (Chicago: Argonaut, 1969), p. 96. See the discussion in M. J. Lagrange, *The Gospel of Jesus Christ* (Westminster, Md.: Newman, 1954), p. xii ("Tacit agreement is of greater value than explicit agreement").

33. Dag Hammarskjold, *Markings,* trans. Leif Sjöberg and W. H. Auden (New York: Knopf, 1964), p. 205.

34. Paul Celan, *Collected Prose,* trans. Rosemarie Waldrop (Manchester, England: Carcanet, 1986), p. 3. (I have changed "the dream about the dream" to "the dream of the dream" as a translation of *der Traum vom Traume.*)

35. Ibid., p. 7. There is a reproduction of this painting, *Ein Segel Verlässt ein Auge,* in *Studio,* vol. 138 (London, 1949), p. 10.

36. Laurens van der Post, *The Heart of the Hunter* (London: Chatto & Windus, 1987), p. 151. See my discussion in *The Reasons of the Heart,* p. 39.

37. Shakespeare, *The Tempest,* act 4, scene 1, line 156.

38. Mario Vargas Llosa, *The Storyteller,* trans. Helen Lane (New York: Farrar Straus Giroux, 1989), p. 127.

39. Revelation 14:2 and 19:6 (King James Version).

40. *Hölderlin,* ed. Michael Hamburger (Baltimore, Md.: Penguin, 1961), p. 203 (my translation).

41. Quoted by Celan, *Collected Prose,* p. 50, "from Malebranche via Walter Benjamin's essay on Kafka."

42. Walter Calé, *Nachgelassene Schriften* (Berlin: S. Fischer, 1914), p. 97. Here is this very lonely poem and my translation:

> Du gabst mir deine Hand, da fühl' ich dich,
> und nichts mehr fühl' ich als den Druck der Hand.
> Denn nur ein Hauch sind deine Worte mir,
> ein toter Hauch, und meine Worte dir;
> und deine Arme, die du um mich schlangest,
> sie spür' ich fern, und deines Lebens Strom,
> der pocht und pocht, verrint mir unerkannt,
> und keine Brücke ist von Mensch zu Mensch.

> You gave me your hand, there I feel you,
> And no more I feel than the pressure of the hand.
> For only a breath are your words to me,
> A dead breath, and my words to you;
> And your arms, that you entwine about me,
> I feel far away, and the river of your life,
> That knocks and knocks, passes me by unrecognized,
> And no bridge is from man to man.

43. Franz Rosenzweig, *The Star of Redemption,* trans. William W. Hallo (New York: Holt, Rinehart & Winston, 1970; rpt. Notre Dame, Ind.: University of Notre Dame Press, 1985), p. 395.

44. Celan, *Collected Prose,* p. 55 (this is from the conclusion of his speech, "The Meridian").

45. "And the bridge is love" is said at the end of Thornton Wilder's story, *The Bridge of San Luis Rey* (New York: Time Inc., 1963), p. 139, and is the title of Alma Mahler Werfel's autobiography in collaboration with E. B. Ashton (New York: Harcourt Brace, 1958). Julia Kristeva poses these questions about the meaning of the word "love" in her *Tales of Love,* trans. Leon S. Roudiez (New York: Columbia University Press, 1987), p. 2.

46. John 21:15–17. The Greek here is

agapas me . . . philo se
agapas me . . . philo se
phileis me . . . philo se

See Raymond E. Brown, *The Gospel According to John (xiii–xxi)* in the Anchor Bible (Garden City, N.Y.: Doubleday, 1970), pp. 1102–3, but I am going here with Ceslas Spicq, *Agape in the New Testament,* vol. 3 (St. Louis & London: Herder, 1966), pp. 94–99, who sees the change of verbs here as significant.

47. Julia Kristeva, *In the Beginning Was Love: Psychoanalysis and Faith,* trans. Arthur Goldhammer (New York: Columbia University Press, 1987).

48. Michel Foucault in *Foucault/Blanchot,* trans. Jeffrey Mehlman and Brian Massumi (New York: Zone Books, 1987), p. 31.

49. I come to this formula in *The House of Wisdom,* p. 135.

50. Celan, *Collected Prose,* p. 49.

51. Foucault in *Foucault/Blanchot,* p. 9.

52. The first translation is by Rosemarie Waldrop in Celan, *Collected Prose,* p. 22. The second is by Katherine Washburn and Margret Guillemin in Celan, *Last Poems,* p. 212. Celan tells about missing the meeting and encountering himself in "The Meridian" in *Collected Prose,* p. 53.

53. The main Psalm to No One is "Psalm" in Celan, *Poems,* trans. Michael Hamburger (New York: Persea Books, 1980), p. 143. "No One" and "Do you hear me?" are in Celan, *Collected Prose,* p. 20 ("Nobody" and "Do you hear me?") and *Last Poems,* p. 210 ("No One" and "Do you

hear?"). "Do you hear me, Lord" is in Perutz, *The Marquis of Bolibar,*
p. 17.

54. Buber said this in the introduction (1909) to his anthology of
mysticism, *Ecstatic Confessions,* ed. Paul Flohr and trans. Esther Cam-
eron (San Francisco: Harper & Row, 1985), p. 7. His later view (1922)
is in *I and Thou,* trans. Ronald Gregor Smith (New York: Scribner's,
1958). See my discussion in *The Homing Spirit* (New York: Crossroad,
1987), p. 56.

55. Tolkien, *The Lord of the Rings,* p. 669.

56. Titus 1:12.

57. John Cage, *Silence* (Middletown, Conn.: Wesleyan University
Press, 1961), p. 3 (this is the opening sentence of his musical credo).

5. The Sense of "I" in Christianity

1. Ray Bradbury, *Dandelion Wine* (New York: Bantam, 1969), p. 7.

2. Diogenes' description of Plato's philosophy in *Herakleitos and Diogenes,* trans. Guy Davenport (San Francisco: Grey Fox, 1983), p. 47
(aphorism #47).

3. Dag Hammarskjold, *Markings,* p. 89.

4. Michel Foucault, *Technologies of the Self,* p. 48.

5. Hammarskjold, "A Room of Quiet: The United Nations Medi-
tation Room," reprinted in Hammarskjold, *Servant of Peace,* ed. Wilder
Foote (London: Bodley Head, 1970), p. 161.

6. Jeff Todd Titon, "The Life Story" in *Journal of American Folklore*
90 (1980): 280.

7. Claude Levi-Strauss, *Myth and Meaning* (New York: Schocken,
1979), pp. 3–4.

8. Martin Buber, *Two Types of Faith* (London: Routledge & Kegan
Paul, 1951), p. 7.

9. David Daube, *New Testament and Rabbinic Judaism* (Salem, N.H.:
Ayer, 1984; reprint of London: Athlone Press, 1956), pp. 325–29.

10. Daube, *Appeasement or Resistance* with subtitle *And Other Essays
in New Testament Judaism* (Berkeley: University of California Press,
1987).

11. Daube, "He That Cometh" (Cowley, Oxford: Church Army
Press, 1966), p. 11.

12. Buber, *Two Types of Faith,* pp. 130ff., 140, 150, 154, 157, 159ff.,
164, 169.

13. John Dominic Crossan, "Divine Immediacy and Human Immediacy" in *Semeia* 44 (1988): 121–40 (especially pp. 125–26).

14. Buber, *I and Thou,* pp. 66–67.

15. Alfred Lord Tennyson, *In Memoriam,* section 97, line 23, ed. Robert H. Ross (New York: Norton, 1973), p. 63.

16. René Girard, *Things Hidden since the Foundation of the World,* trans. by Stephen Bann and Michael Metteer (Stanford, Ca.: Stanford University Press, 1987), pp. 180–223.

17. Martin Heidegger, *Being and Time,* trans. John Macquarrie and Edward Robinson (New York: Harper, 1962), p. 284.

18. 2 Corinthians 5:14 (King James Version).

19. Girard, *The Scapegoat,* trans. Yvonne Freccero (Baltimore: Johns Hopkins University Press, 1986), p. 200.

20. Simone Weil, *Gravity and Grace* (London & New York: Ark, 1987), p. 117.

21. John 18:37.

22. Heidegger, *loc. cit.*

23. Erik Erikson, *The Life Cycle Completed* (New York: Norton, 1985), p. 62. See p. 86 on translating Freud's "Ich" as "I" rather than "ego."

24. Matthew 26:39, Mark 14:36 (cf. Luke 22:42).

25. Erikson, *The Life Cycle Completed,* p. 87.

26. Erikson, "The Galilean Sayings and the Sense of 'I'" in *Yale Review,* Spring 1981, pp. 321–62.

27. Ibid., p. 358. Cf. my discussion in my book *The House of Wisdom,* p. 133.

28. Ephesians 3:17.

29. Galatians 2:20.

30. See my discussion of this sentence in *The House of Wisdom,* p. 21.

31. G. K. Chesterton, *Saint Thomas Aquinas 'The Dumb Ox'* (Garden City, N.Y.: Doubleday Image, 1956), p. 143.

32. John 17:23. Cf. Buber, *I and Thou,* p. 85, where he calls John "the Gospel of pure relation."

6. The Peace of the Present

1. I am grateful to Father William Botzum, C.S.C., for pointing out this saying to me in Tihamer Toth, *The Great Teacher,* trans. V. G. Agotai, ed. Newton Thompson (London: Herder, 1939), p. 129. See the discussion of it by Kenneth Cragg, *Jesus and the Muslim* (London:

Allen & Unwin, 1985), p. 47, and by Joachim Jeremias, *Unknown Sayings of Jesus,* trans. R. H. Fuller (London: SPCK, 1964), pp. 111–18.

2. Celan, "The Meridian" in *Collected Prose,* p. 49.

3. Leon Bloy, *Pilgrim of the Absolute,* selections by Raissa Maritain, trans. John Coleman and Harry Lorin Binsse (New York: Pantheon, 1947), p. 349. Graham Greene uses this saying as the epigraph of his novel *The End of the Affair* (New York: Viking, 1951), p. 1.

4. See Leo Bersani and Ulysse Dutoit, *The Forms of Violence* (New York: Schocken, 1985), especially the chapters on "narrativity and violence," pp. 40–56, and "the restlessness of desire," pp. 110–25.

5. Tolkien, *The Lord of the Rings,* pp. 48, 86, and 1024.

6. Heidegger poses this question (from Leibniz) in his *Introduction to Metaphysics,* trans. Ralph Manheim (New Haven, Conn.: Yale University Press, 1959), p. 1.

7. Wordsworth uses this expression in his preface to *Lyrical Ballads,* in *William Wordsworth: Selected Prose,* ed. John O. Hayden (New York: Penguin, 1988), p. 297.

8. Shakespeare, *The Tempest,* act 1, scene 2, lines 45 and 49–50. See my discussion in *A Search for God in Time and Memory,* p. 211.

9. Ibid., act 5, scene 1, lines 18–20.

10. Ibid., lines 50–51.

11. Ibid., Epilogue, lines 1–3 and 15–17.

12. Hannah Arendt, *On Violence* (New York: Harcourt, Brace & World, 1970), pp. 44–46 (here she defines power, strength, force, authority, and violence).

13. Montague John Rendall wrote this as the motto of the BBC in 1927.

14. See Matthew 7:12 and Luke 6:31.

15. Shakespeare, *The Tempest,* act 1, scene 2, lines 375–76.

16. Ibid., lines 397–402.

17. Milton Avery as quoted by Barbara Haskell, *Milton Avery* (New York: Whitney Museum with Harper & Row, 1982), p. 12 (epigraph of the book).

18. Tolkien, *The Lord of the Rings,* p. 1066.

19. Milton Avery as quoted by Una E. Johnson, *Milton Avery* (Brooklyn, N.Y.: Brooklyn Museum, 1966), p. 10.

20. "East o' the Sun and West o' the Moon" is the title of the tale in Stith Thompson, *One Hundred Favorite Folktales* (Bloomington: Indiana University Press, 1974), pp. 113–21.

21. Mercer Mayer, *East of the Sun and West of the Moon* (New York:

Macmillan, 1980), last sentence (pages not numbered). The original version ends rather differently, saying the prince and the princess "flitted away as far as they could from the castle that lay East o' the Sun and West o' the Moon" (Stith Thompson, *One Hundred Favorite Folktales,* p. 122). I see here a mixture of dread and fascination, as in Yeats' play, *The Land of Heart's Desire.*

22. Shakespeare, *The Tempest,* act 4, scene 1, lines 156–57 and 162–63.

23. See my discussion of the infinite sphere at the end of *The Way of All the Earth,* p. 232.

24. Donna Cohen and Carl Eisdorfer, *Loss of Self* ("A Family Resource for the Care of Alzheimer's Disease and Related Disorders") (New York: New American Library, 1986).

25. John 11:25–26.

26. Gilles Deleuze and Felix Guattari, *Nomadology: The War Machine,* trans. Brian Massumi (New York: Semiotext, 1986), pp. 1 and 49. The nomads are the heroes in this essay taken from the larger work by Deleuze and Guattari, *A Thousand Plateaus* (Minneapolis: University of Minnesota Press, 1987).

27. Dag Hammarskjold, *Markings,* p. 90.

28. Arthur Rimbaud, *Oeuvres,* ed. by Paul Hartmann (Strasbourg: Broceliande, 1957), p. 292 (his letter to George Izambard, May 13, 1871). See the discussion in George Steiner, *Real Presences* (Chicago: University of Chicago Press, 1989), p. 99.

29. Evan S. Connell, *A Long Desire* (San Francisco: North Point, 1988).

Index

Adorno, Theodore, 73–74, 77
Agape, 87
Anatta (no self), 93
Apocalpytic faith, 41–49
Arendt, Hannah, 30–31, 106
Assurance, 50. *See also* uncertainty
Attention as natural prayer of the soul, 88, 104–5
Augustine, 22, 24, 25–26, 31, 32, 73
Autonomy, 60
Avery, Milton, 108, 109

Baal Shem Tov, 7
Bach, J. S., 13–14
Bachelard, Gaston, 39, 48–49
Bellah, Robert: *Habits of the Heart*, 71
Benjamin, Walter, 104–5
Bhagavad Gita, 34–40, 106
Blixen, Karen. *See* Dinesen, Isak
Bloy, Leon, 103
Bonhoeffer, Dietrich, 4
Bradbury, Ray: *Dandelion Wine*, 92, 99
Buber, Martin, 7, 11, 35, 37, 90, 92, 94, 95, 100

Buddhism
    Center as stillness and silence, 101
    God as void, 68
    No self, doctrine of, 93
    Willingness to die, 36, 40

Cage, John, 91
Cain and Abel, 24, 28
Calderón, Pedro: *Life Is a Dream*, 74–75, 85
Calé, Walter, 86
Celan, Paul, 70, 83–84, 88, 89, 102, 104–5
Cendrars, Blaise, 78
Chesterton, G. K., 100
Christ. *See* Jesus Christ
Claudel, Paul, 43–44
Conrad, Joseph, 12
Contemplation
    End of desire, 3–4
    Thinking and loving, 55
    Unity of life in prayer, 104–5

Dark Night of the Soul, 72
Daube, David, 92–95, 98, 100–101
Death
    Accepting death in advance, 36

Death (*cont.*)
  Accepting death, life dissolves
    into eternal, 79–80
  Fear of, 4–5, 36
  Grasping desire as cause of
    wasting death, 12
  Heidegger, certainty of death,
    96, 97, 111
  "I will die," loneliness shared
    with Christ, 95–97
  Rejoining the whole, 57–59
  Willingness to die, 70
Descartes, René, 96
Desire
  Beginning of desire, 2, 12–21
  End of desire, 2–12
  End of desire as beginning of
    desire, 103–4
  Mimetic violence, xi
  Substitution in desire result-
    ing in violence, 96–97
  Ways of desire, 1–21
  See also Heart's desire; Mi-
    metic desire; Nonviolence
Dinesen, Isak, 42–43, 54, 66–67
Dissonance, perceived before
  harmony, 86
Doolittle, Hilda, 16, 17
Dream, life as, 74–75, 84–85,
  110
Dürrenmatt, Friedrich, 31

Eckhart, Meister, 18, 47, 99
Einstein, Alfred, 31
Eliot, T. S., 69
Ellis-Fermor, Una, 14
Epimenides, 90
Erikson, Erik, 14, 92, 97–99,
  100, 101
Eros, 87

Faith and faithfulness, 52–53,
  62–63
Fear and fearing, 2, 4–5, 36
Foucault, Michel, 88, 89, 93
Freud, Sigmund, 9, 11, 110

Gandhi, Mohandes
  Eventual triumph of truth
    and love, 33–34
  Impersonality of God, 51
  Need for spiritual discipline
    for nonviolence, 23
  Satyagraha, 34–40
Geronimo, 73
Girard, René
  Coquetry, 11
  Desire and violence as mi-
    metic, xi, 2
  Desire has no content, 24–25
  "I" in Christianity, 92, 95–97,
    100–101
  Metaphysical desire, 8
  Origins of world, 25
  Renunciation of all violence,
    40
  Violence as mimetic, 22
  Violent origins of humanity,
    23
Gita. *See* Bhagavad Gita
Glass, Philip: *Satyagraha*, 34
God
  Alone and unalone, 11
  As observer or observed, 32
  Boundless mercy, 44, 65
  Coming of God, 66–68
  Common good, God in us as,
    38–39
  Dios lo quiere, 62–63, 65
  Dios viene, 66, 68
  God's fool, 51, 52, 69–70

God (*cont.*)
  Immediacy of Jesus with, 94
  Immediacy toward God, 73, 95
  One who shines, 47–48
  Peace of the present, ix
  The divider, 47
  Unity of, 41
  Waiting on God. *See* Love, Waiting on
  Whole, God identical with, 58
Goethe, J. W., 28, 33, 41
Grace, 68, 101
Graves, Robert, 82
Guss, David, 71–72

Hammarskjold, Dag, 83, 93
Hardening of one's heart. *See* Violence
Harmony, 59, 82–86, 90–91, 110. *See also* Dissonance
Harper, Ralph, 17
H. D. *See* Doolittle, Hilda
Heart's desire
  Absence or presence, 107
  Desiring what is not known, 13
  God unrecognized as, 25–26, 108
  Land of, 1
  Living someone else's story, 80–81
  Mimetic desire distinguished from, ix, 22
  Preparedness for life, 81
  Story giving expression to, 103–4
  Working through mimetic desire, 33

Heart-whole, 80–81
Hegel, G. W. F., 33
Heidegger, Martin
  Disclosing being in naming, 27
  "I will die," certainty of, 96, 97, 111
  Letting be, 10, 18
  Salvation and danger from same source, 79
  Waiting, silence, and mystery, 54–56
Heraclitus, 83
Hinduism
  God dwells within you, 100
  Vedanta, 15
  See also Bhagavad Gita
Hölderin, Friedrich
  God cannot be grasped alone, 85–86
  Heart desires too much, 74, 80–81
  Salvation and danger having same source, 76–77
  Solitude of time, 78–80
  Time as opaque, 81–82
Homer: *Iliad*, 48, 106
Hope, 68–69, 97–99
Horney, Karen, 27

"I" in Christianity
  Christ dwelling within, 99–100
  Consciousness of Jesus, 95
  Daube, David, 92–95, 98, 100–101
  Erikson, Erik, 92, 97–99, 100–101
  Girard, René, 92, 95–97, 100–101

"I" in Christianity (*cont.*)
  Hollow self, I as, 93
  "I am" sayings of Jesus, 39, 93–95, 98
  "I am with you," 97–99
  "I" as relationship and in-dwelling, 101
  "I will die," 95–97
  Locus of peace, 92
  Personal and transcendent "I am," 98–99
  Presence of God within, 94–95
  Will, I linked with, 92–93
Iliad, 48, 106
Individual, emergence and separation of, 71
Indwelling of Christ, 99–101, 112. *See also* Shekinah
Irarrazaval, Diego, xi
Isaiah, 72

Jameson, Anna, 9
Jené, Edgar, 83–84
Jesus Christ
  "I am" sayings, 39, 93–95, 98
  Imitation as pursuit of beloved, 14, 16
  Indwelling. *See* Indwelling of Christ
  Peace of Christ incompatible with use of force, 46
  Resurrection, 96
  Violence of society revealed in Christ as victim, 95–97
Job, 46
John of the Cross, Saint, 72
Jonah, 44

Kafka, Franz, 82
Kant, Immanuel, 41
Karma, 30
Kenyatta, Jomo, 67
Khan, Badshah, 39, 40
Kierkegaard, Søren
  Falling spider parable, 29–30, 32
  Individualism, 73
  Longing as anxiety, 76
King, Martin Luther, 34, 38–40
Kristeva, Julia, 87, 88

Lawrence, T. E., 23
Letting go, 5–6, 75–77. *See also* Renunciation
Levi-Strauss, Claude, 93
Lifton, Robert Jay, xi, 9, 46
Llosa, Mario Vargas, 85
Logue, Christopher, 23
Loneliness
  Boundless mercy of God, 65
  God who reintegrates, 48
  Grace touching loneliness, 101
  Heart's desire experienced as, 1–2
  "I will die," loneliness of, 97–98
  Leading to heart's desire, 114
  Letting go and emergence, 75–77
  Love transforming loneliness, 56
  Loving in desolation resulting in faith, 63
  Necessary for discovering God, 9
  New name, 6–7
  Waiting on God's love, 52–53

Love
    Christ revealing uncondi-
      tional love of God, 97
    Desire for, 1
    Direction, love as, 61–62, 68–
      69
    Eros, Agape, Philia, 87
    Eventual triumph of truth
      and love, 33–34
    Faithfulness to heart's desire,
      107
    Learning to love, 22
    Mimetic desire changing to
      heart's desire, 21
    Necessary for nonviolence,
      23, 26–27
    State of soul, 62
    Transforming loneliness, 56
    Waiting on love, 51–70
Luke, Helen, xi, 22

MacDonald, George, 6–7, 8, 14
Malebranche, Nicholas de, 104
Malraux, André, 79
Marcel, Gabriel, 46
Mary and Martha, 55, 56
Melville, Herman, 46
Memory
    From memory to understand-
      ing to will, 88
    Love, remembering and for-
      getting, 62, 70
    Memento mori, 5
    Moving from violence to non-
      violence, 105–8
    Origin of personal world, 25
Merton, Thomas, 11–12, 13
Mimetic desire
    Desiring what is known, 13
    Girard on, ix, 2

Mimetic desire (*cont.*)
    Heart's desire distinguished
      from, ix, 22
    Heart's desire prior to knowl-
      edge, 25
    Story giving expression to,
      103–4
Mistral, Gabriela: *Dios Lo Quiere,*
    62
Mystery
    Containing meaning, 12
    Encounter, mystery of, 88
    God as end of desire, 7
    Letting be, 10–11
    Love's substance, 108
    Openness to God, 16
    Openness to mystery, 56
    Rahner on, 64–65
    Resurrection as mystery of
      faith, 96
    Violence resulting from ab-
      sence of mystery, 105
Myth. *See* Story

Naming, new name, 6–7, 26–
    28
Neruda, Pablo, 12
Nietzsche, Friedrich, 44
Nonviolence
    Heart's desire as source, 22–
      23
    See also Violence
Numbing the heart
    Violence as, xi
    Suffering from heart's numb-
      ness, 103

O'Connor, Flannery: *The Violent
    Bear It Away,* 63–64

Parousia, 44

Parra, Nicandor, 11

Participation

Christ and human disappearing within each other, 101

Substitution and, 96–97

Understanding leading to
will, 15

Passing over and returning to
self

Bridge to God and others,
87–91, 100, 102–4

Intimacy and distance, 99

Transcendence of longing, 77

Paul, 6, 99

Peace

Faith as seeing peace of God,
50

"I" as locus of, 92, 113

Peaceable kingdom, 71–91

Peace of Christ, 46

Peace of the Present, vii, ix,
102–14

Perutz, Leo, 51–53, 55–62, 66–
68

Peter, 6, 88

Philia, 87

Plato, 87

Prayer

Attention as natural prayer of
soul, 88, 104–5

Unity of all life in, 18–20

See also Contemplation

Proust, Marcel, 64

Rahner, Karl, 64–66

Renunciation

End of desire, fulfillment, 3–4

Letting go and receiving, 5–6

Path to center of desire, 2

Restlessness

Desire's restlessness, 28–29,
78, 104

Direction of love, 108

Longing for home, 102

Resting in the restless movement of the heart, 61

Violence and unviolence, 28–
29

Resurrection as mystery of faith,
96

Ribeiro, Joao Ubalso, 43

Rilke, Rainer Maria, 49

Rimbaud, Arthur, 113

Rodin, Auguste, 14

Romulus and Remus, 24, 28

Rosenzweig, Franz, 86

Sartre, Jean Paul, 7

Satan, 41

Satyagraha, 34–40

Schürmann, Reiner, 28

Shakespeare, William, ix, 24,
85, 103, 106, 110

Shaw, George Bernard, 4

Shekinah

Jesus, "I am," 111

Presence of God, 94–95, 98

Silence

Center of stillness and silence, 112–13

Mystery of, 100, 101

Presence in, 93

Waiting, silence, and mystery,
54–55

Smuts, Jan, 35, 40

Solovyov, Vladimir, 45–46

Song of Solomon, 51, 70

Steere, Douglas, 19

Steinbeck, John, 82

Steiner, George, 18
Stillness. *See* Silence
Story
    Expressing mimetic desire,
      103–4
    Four cycles, 71–72
    Immortal story, 42–43
    Myth and, 24, 72
    Story of story, 83–84
    Unknown ending, 109

Tagore, Rabindranath, 34, 37
Talmud, 18
Thinking is thanking, 18–19
Thomas à Kempis, 14
Tocqueville, Alexis de, 71
Tolkien, J. R. R., 5, 32, 42, 71,
    82–83, 90, 104, 109
Tolstoy, Leo
    God is my desire, 18, 40, 104,
      108
    Kingdom of God is within,
      44–45
    Violence to nonviolence, 41
    War and Peace, x, 41, 106

Unamuno, Miguel de, 43
Uncertainty, 44, 49–50, 53
Union and reunion
    Alone and unalone, 11–12
    God, ix
    God's love, 109
    Heart's desire, 1–2
    Road of union of love with
      God, 72
    Waiting on God's love, 53

Valery, Paul, 59–60
Van der Post, Laurens, 84

Vedanta, 15
Villon, Francois, 56–57
Violence
    Contemplation's absence, 105
    Holding on and letting go,
      74–75
    Psychic numbing, 46–47
    Violence arising from "I is an
      other," 113
    Violence of society revealed
      in Christ as victim, 95–97
    Violent and unviolent ways,
      22–50

War, war music, x, 36–37, 106
Weil, Simone
    Attention as natural prayer of
      the soul, 104–5
    Desolation, faith as loving
      God in, 62–63, 65
    Force as numbing, 33
    God who reintegrates, 48
    Grace fills empty spaces, 68
    Hidden needs and thoughts,
      71
    Love as direction, 61, 68–69
    Mysteries of faith, 96
Whitehead, Alfred North, 20,
    23
Whitman, Walt, 58
Wholeness, 15–16
Will
    Conflict of God's and human's
      will, 65–66
    Giving up will for reunion
      with God, 110–11
    "I" linked with, 92–93
    Willingness and hope, 68–69
    Willingness to die and love,
      56–58, 70

Williams, Charles, 4, 8
Word
    Hidden harmony of I and
        thou, 90–91

Word (*cont.*)
    Trust in, 27–31
Wright, A. T., 34

Yeats, Y. B., 1, 2, 60